INTENTIONAL

INTENTIONAL

Getting Past Multigen Worship

DAVID A. TATUM

WIPF & STOCK · Eugene, Oregon

INTENTIONAL
Getting Past Multigen Worship

Copyright © 2026 David A. Tatum. All rights reserved. Except for brief quotations in critical publications or reviews, no part of this book may be reproduced in any manner without prior written permission from the publisher. Write: Permissions, Wipf and Stock Publishers, 199 W. 8th Ave., Suite 3, Eugene, OR 97401.

Wipf & Stock
An Imprint of Wipf and Stock Publishers
199 W. 8th Ave., Suite 3
Eugene, OR 97401

www.wipfandstock.com

PAPERBACK ISBN: 979-8-3852-5985-4
HARDCOVER ISBN: 979-8-3852-5986-1
EBOOK ISBN: 979-8-3852-5987-8

01/05/26

Scripture quotations are from the ESV® Bible (The Holy Bible, English Standard Version˚, copyright © 2001 by Crossway, a publishing ministry of Good News Publishers. Used by permission. All rights reserved.

To Denise,
without you, this project would not have been possible,

and to Garrett, Jaden, Tyson, Natalie, Kenzie, Edmund, and Corinne,
you are the next generations of worshipers.

Contents

Acknowledgments | ix

1 Introduction | 1

Part One: What Does the Bible Say About Intergenerational Worship? | 11

2 The Old Testament | 14

3 The Psalms | 42

4 The New Testament | 50

Part Two: Why Does Worshiping Intergenerationally Really Matter? | 65

5 What Is Intergenerational Worship? | 67

6 What's Really at Stake? | 74

7 What Does Being Intentional Look Like? | 82

8 Making the Big Shift: Reviving God's Plan for Worship | 103

Part Three: How Can I Be Intentionally Intergenerational in Worship? | 115

9 Planning for Intergenerational Worship | 117

10 Leading Intergenerational Worship | 124

11 Resources for Being Intentionally Intergenerational in Worship | 130

Appendix: The Creative Worship Task Force | 155

Bibliography | 159

Acknowledgments

Having served in the local church for over thirty years, I have been able to see many changes in the landscape of corporate worship. This volume is the culmination of thoughts, plans, and dreams through a lifetime of ministry. I began this journey in the 1990s in a small West Texas town and have seen God lead us through many different ministries and into two different states.

There have been incredible educators who have poured into me and helped to shape my concepts of both music and worship. Loyd Hawthorne, Larry Wolz, Andrew J. Patterson, Bruce Leafblad, A. Joseph King, C. David Keith, R. Allen Lott, Rhonda Edge Buescher, Angela Cofer, William J. Reynolds, and James McKinney set high standards and goals for ministry, and I have sought to use their sage advice and instruction throughout the years. I am especially grateful to Scott Aniol and David Toledo for helping shape my thinking on how intergenerational worship fits into the broader picture of the church at large. Words could never fully express my gratitude to Joseph Crider for the countless hours of reading and encouragement.

To all the staffs and congregations of the churches I have been privileged to serve, I am thankful that you encouraged me and allowed me to both lead you and learn from you. To my pastor and friend, Richard Lee, thank you for the many hours of encouragement and discussions of weighty theological concepts.

I am also grateful to be part of an incredible legacy of faithfulness. My family is one in which the concepts of Psalm 145:4 were truly lived out. I am thankful for great-grandparents, grandparents, aunts, uncles, and parents who saw the need and the responsibility to live faithful lives of worship in front of me. I am grateful for a father, D. Vaughn Tatum, who continues to model the life of a worshiper and a minister so well. I am also thankful for my mother, Kathy Tatum, who always encourages me to seek after my

Acknowledgments

dreams and God's best. I am thankful to have joined a family through marriage that has much the same legacy of faith with in-laws who are actively involved in vocational ministry and serving God daily.

Most importantly, I am thankful for my wife, Denise. Thank you for the times spent dreaming dreams of ministry, for times spent weeping over hurts, and for times spent rejoicing over victories. Without you, a life of ministry would not have been possible. I am so grateful for your willingness to sacrifice much so we could do what God called us to do. I am also grateful that we can partner in life and in parenting. Garrett, Jaden, Tyson, Natalie, and Kenzie—anytime I think of intergenerational worship, I think of you and how each of you is actively involved in worship in your churches. I am also grateful that you are exercising the teaching of Deuteronomy 6 with the next generation in Edmund and Corinne.

Finally, I am thankful to God for his provision and guidance. I am thankful that, though knowing man would fall, he provided a way for us to reconnect and commune with him in worship. His design of family and church offer innumerable ways to be spiritually transformed into the likeness of Christ.

1

Introduction

IT IS SUNDAY MORNING, and the aroma of coffee fills the air. There are shouted greetings and a buzz of conversation as happy people see each other for the first time in a week. Children dart through the crowd on their way to their ministry areas. Sleepy teenagers stop by the coffee station for a dose of caffeine before trudging their way to the student area upstairs. Parents wave goodbye to their children and enter the auditorium for a time of worship as the senior adults exit following their traditional service.

A similar scene is repeated in many churches across America each week; multiple generations gathered in one place yet disconnected from each other. They attend different worship services separated by time, musical style, dress codes, and ultimately congregant age. In many situations, each of these worship services begin to function as entirely separate congregations worshiping under one roof. Children are discipled by children's ministry leaders in Bible study and then participate in high-energy, fun-filled worship times specifically geared to their developmental age and stage. Students participate in Bible study and "appropriate" age-oriented worship led by select volunteers or their peers. College students gather with other young singles for a modern worship encounter. Parents experience worship and Bible study in an atmosphere tailored to their needs and interests. Senior adults join with other seniors and enjoy traditional worship that evokes a sense of nostalgia. Often, families separate as they leave their cars in the parking lot, only to regather once the morning's events are complete. But is this scenario what God intended when he instituted the family and created the church?

Intentional

God's Plan for Worship

Scripture is full of instruction regarding how we should worship. Over and over, God tells his people to seriously and intentionally invest their lives in discipling the next generation. Nowhere is this mandate more evident than in Ps 145. Here, David proclaims that God's plan is for one generation to commend his works to subsequent generations. The way we are currently "doing church" has made fulfilling this God-given task very difficult to accomplish. Churches have compartmentalized the generations in Bible study, discipleship, fellowship, evangelism, ministry, and in many cases even worship.[1] Noted Christian theologian John Witvliet states, "For the past several decades, many North American congregations have pursued generationally segregated approaches to worship and church life."[2] Witvliet goes on to say that as churches give in to popular cultural patterns of separating people by age, they risk reimagining the way we worship on its most basic level. Churches may see an opportunity to focus on, or target, a single generation as a way to encourage numerical growth—but if they do so, those churches may give up any possibility of learning across multiple generations.[3] But God has shown us a better way in Scripture.

As God commanded through the psalmist, it is his plan for one generation to teach his works, his character, and his nature to each succeeding generation. If we eliminate the possibility of intergenerational interactions in worship by intentionally—or even unintentionally—segregating our congregations by age, we also eliminate almost every opportunity for one generation to speak into the lives of others. What's more, even in congregations where multiple generations are usually present in the weekly worship gathering, there may be little, if any, intentional interaction between the people. Being intergenerational requires more than just being together, breathing the same air, and filling the same space. To move beyond simply being in the same place at the same time, we must be intentional in the ways

---

1. Allen and Ross state that in the past one hundred years, societal changes resulting in age segregation due to public education, new-found mobility of families, transition from extended to nuclear families, and the rise of preschools and nursing homes, have begun to take hold in faith communities to the point that "in the second decade of twenty-first century America, all generations of the faith community—babies through nonagenarians—are seldom together." Allen and Ross, *Intergenerational Christian Formation*, 30–31.

2. Witvliet, *Nursery of the Holy Spirit*, ix.

3. Witvliet, *Nursery of the Holy Spirit*, ix.

Introduction

our people interact with all the other generations. How well the different generations interact will determine how well our churches can follow God's command and commend his works from one generation to another.

MULTIGENERATIONAL VS. INTERGENERATIONAL

The concept of an intergenerational church is nothing new. I grew up in the home of a Southern Baptist music minister in the 1970s. The churches that we attended and served were distinctly intergenerational. When you walked into worship each Sunday, you would find children, youth, adults, and senior adults. There always seemed to be a sense of everyone pulling together. Since both my parents were on the platform during the service, Dad leading the music and Mom in the choir, my siblings and I sat with adopted aunts, uncles, and grandparents—each of them helping us to understand our place and our role in worship. They were intentional in teaching us the ways in which we could participate in worship. I learned that there were times I should sing God's praises at the top of my lungs, and there were times to sit in awe and wonder as I pondered the nature, character, and wondrous works of God. I learned to hear and truly treasure the reading of God's word, and it was in those moments that I began to hide its words in my heart. I learned what it meant to pray for others, for my church, for my country, and for my family. Most of all, I learned that I had a place and a purpose in worship—that even as a child, God had created, called, and commanded *me* to worship. These lessons and others I learned from those older adults still affect the way that I worship some fifty years later. Now, as a parent and grandparent myself, I see even more clearly the impact that I could have on the future generations of my family. I can also now see the influence my children's offerings of worship have had in my life.

The sad truth today is that in many churches, the concept of generations worshiping and growing together has all but disappeared. What used to be so common that we did not even think about it has changed to a sense of unease or even distaste as the various generations may be thrust together in a worship service. Because of a sensitive situation just this week, my pastor and I were visiting about the issue of age segregation in worship. This past Sunday, our church experienced a wonderful service full of children and babies. It was nothing out of the ordinary, but the children may have been a little more rambunctious than normal. Later in the week, a long-time church member proclaimed that she didn't want those crying babies interfering in her worship service—they were interrupting her focus and her peace of mind. She couldn't understand the importance of those babies being in worship. As a predictable result of that kind of self-serving attitude, in many churches, preschoolers and early school-age children are left in an extended teaching session through both the Bible study hour and the worship service. Older children may then graduate to children's church. As they continue to age, the segregation becomes even more entrenched as students sit together in the balcony or the last few rows of the worship center. There is a definite separation—a segregation—of the generations. Truly intergenerational churches that were once so common have been replaced by multigenerational churches seeking to be developmentally appropriate, culturally relevant, and, dare I say, self-serving country clubs.

So, what do I mean by describing churches as either multigenerational or intergenerational? There is a distinct difference between these two models. A multigenerational church may have several generations present, but unlike the churches in which I grew up, there is no connection or interaction between the age groups. The generations may be separated in almost every aspect of the church's ministry, from Bible study to fellowship and worship. Multigenerational churches could even become separate age-segregated congregations simply worshiping under the same roof during a weekend. Multigenerational church members may travel to church together, but that's where the togetherness ends. On the other hand, an intergenerational church intentionally focuses on creating interconnected relationships between members of different generations.[4] In other words, an intergenerational church seeks out ways to connect the generations, much like my adopted aunts, uncles, and grandparents did when I was a child.

I could guess that many churches across the country are probably multigenerational, but how many are truly intergenerational? How many are seeking to be *intentionally* intergenerational? This book seeks to change the answers to these questions by describing how worship leaders and pastors

---

4. The definition of intergenerational used in this book is derived from a synthesis of three definitions by different scholars. Allen and Ross, *Intergenerational Christian Formation*, 19, state that an intergenerational church deliberately "cultivates meaningful interaction between generations." See also Harkness, "Intergenerational and Homogeneous-Age Education," 52, who offers that intergenerationality "encourages interpersonal interactions across generational boundaries." Finally, see White, *Intergenerational Religious Education*, 18, who proclaims that to be intergenerational, there must be "two or more different age groups of people in a religious community together learning/growing/living in faith through in-common sharing."

Introduction

can design worship services that help to transform a church from being simply multigenerational to being fully and intentionally intergenerational.

At this point, you may think that it is all doom and gloom, but there is a glimmer of hope. There is a new resurgence of interest in intentionally putting the generations back together, and one segment of church ministry leaders have recently been seeking to make changes in how the generations interact with each other. Over the past several years, worship leaders have sought to bring the generations together through the concept of multigenerational worship.

Multigen Worship

There is a "new" buzzword receiving an incredible amount of traction in worship leadership circles today: multigenerational worship, or simply multigen worship. Churches who have become generationally disconnected are beginning to seek out ways to reconnect, and multigen worship is one avenue leaders are using to see integration begin. Howard Vanderwell, former professor at Calvin Seminary, states that "the recent history of generational segregation seems to have generated quite a hunger for intergenerational community in which children and older adults (and everyone in between) can be blessed by the presence of each other."[5] The concept of multigen worship carries with it the idea that multiple generations will not only worship together but will help to lead in worship.

Even a cursory glance at recent offerings from mainstream church music publishers shows a renewed focus on multigen worship. New songs tagged with the multigenerational label are being produced at an incredible pace. For a product/song to be considered multigenerational it must include ways to involve multiple generations. A multigen song may have parts for any combination of adult, student, or children's choirs. Many resources also offer opportunities for soloists or readers of differing generations. Products specifically designated as multigenerational are becoming a larger share of the church music market today. For example, at LifeWay Worship, sales of choral anthems with a multigenerational focus were consistently outperforming almost all others at a rate of nearly two to one at

---

5. Vanderwell, *Church of All Ages*, xii. See also Allen, *InterGenerate*, 17; Penner, *Youth Worker's Guide*, 1; Jones, *Perspectives on Family Ministry*, 1–3; White, *Intergenerational Religious Education*, 1; Baucham, *Family Driven Faith*, 213; Haynes, *Shift*, 30; and Menconi, *Intergenerational Church*, 4–5.

the time of this writing.⁶ As a result, many music publishers have developed entire genres or series of music designated as "Multigen."⁷ While these forays into multigen worship can be a very useful and impactful resource, how we choose to implement these products in our churches may be limiting true intergenerationality.

Intergenerational ministry scholars Holly Allen and Christine Ross say that to be truly intergenerational in focus, a ministry must set as a primary objective the intentional interaction between members of various generations.⁸ In most churches utilizing multigen music, they are simply incorporating the children and/or students to either observe or perform for a certain service or instance, but they are not encouraging these emerging generations to participate in the overarching fabric of the church's worship life. In other words, children and students perform their designated music and are then quickly shuffled off the platform to become mere spectators for the remainder of the service, or until the next opportunity for a multigen service arises.

In my ministry, I wholeheartedly joined in this same process. We incorporated several times of multigen worship through our church year. We ordered the music. Our children, students, and adults rehearsed their parts—all in their separate, age-segregated rehearsals. The week before the service that was to feature the multigen aspect, we brought everyone together for a final rehearsal. Our children had their place on the platform, our students moved into their designated spots, and the adults stayed in their normal place in the choir loft. We were having a moment of multigenerational participation, yet we were still segregated—in rehearsals, in scheduling, and even by physical placement on the platform. After several attempts at trying this type of multigenerational worship moment, we realized that there must be a better way to integrate those on the platform.

---

6. Craig Adams, conversation with author, January 15, 2021. The designation of a multigenerational anthem is contingent on the usage of multiple age groups (e.g., adult choirs, student choirs, children's choirs), soloists, and readers.

7. LifeWay MG (Multigenerational) Series, Houston's First Baptist Church for Multigenerational Worship Series, Brentwood-Benson (MG) Multigeneration Series.

8. Allen and Ross state that "intergenerational ministry occurs when a congregation intentionally brings the generations together in mutual serving, sharing, or learning within the core activities of the church in order to live out being the body of Christ to each other and the greater community." The sense of intentional mutuality is essential in this process—without it a church is simply multigenerational in nature. Allen and Ross, *Intergenerational Christian Formation*, 17.

Introduction

A few years ago, I met with the leaders of the children and student ministries in our church. I was able to get buy-in from our children's leadership for a new way of doing multigen worship. In lieu of the normal children and adult choir rehearsals and other activities during the summer months, we decided that we would meet together. So, for ten weeks, our children and adults met every Wednesday evening for an hour and a half. The adults changed the way that they normally rehearsed. The children also made drastic changes in what their summer activities usually looked like. We fellowshipped together. We ate together. We worshiped together. We rehearsed together. We even played silly games together. In fact, one of my favorite pictures from that first summer was one of our sweet senior adult ladies with her hands behind her back, competing with a third grader by trying to eat a donut suspended from the ceiling on a string. We learned something very important from those moments together. We learned that when you spend time together, sacrificing your own preferences and doing things in which the other generations might fully engage, you begin to build connections that can pay huge benefits. Yes, we used some incredible multigen worship resources from the major publishers, but we changed the focus of *how* we used them. We didn't focus on the music per se, we focused on building relationships. As we did so, we were also able to use songs from gifted composers and arrangers to make beautiful music together as we rehearsed.

We spent the summer working toward presenting a morning of worship. We then shared it on a Sunday just after school began in the fall. We were very intentional about how we implemented our plan. We didn't have special places for the adults or children to stand—we integrated everyone together in the choir loft. Children were interspersed among the adults, and we constantly changed where everyone was seated. It may have been difficult for that one bass who has been sitting in the same chair since before most of the rest of the folks present were born. But as each generation sacrificed and made changes to accommodate and incorporate the others, they began to forge relationships that will continue long after the summer rehearsals come to an end. More than that, they were learning how to worship together!

What are some of the benefits that our church has seen from that multigenerational summer? When we spent time together, we found that we craved more time together. Months later, after we reverted to our normal, age-segregated schedule, we were still seeing children come up and join us in the choir loft during our weekly worship services. They felt as if they belonged there. They felt loved and supported by adults in the music and worship ministry. If they didn't come on the platform, they participated in worship with more intention and more heart because a connection had been made. When we passed each other in the church hallways, there was deep communication that now happened where once there was a shallow hello at most. By intentionally focusing on this time, we saw a dramatic change in the way our church worshiped. By the way, our one-year experiment has now turned into multiple years of spending the summers together.

Making this adjustment is not for the faint of heart. If we choose to be intergenerational, we must intently and intentionally focus on being intergenerational. A more drastic divide can occur if we half-heartedly or indiscriminately involve emerging generations in worship leadership. When we sparingly use children and students in worship leadership rather than consistently and intentionally incorporating them, our congregations begin to see them more as performers rather than worship leaders. Howard Vanderwell contends that children leading in worship tend to be considered "cute" by the more mature worshipers. He states that:

> When our responses signal to them [children leading worship] that we expect them to be "cute" rather than an intrinsic part of the drama of worship, we may have missed their contribution to the dialogue between God and God's people. Our responses to what we perceive as "cuteness" may seem appropriate at the time, but may cheapen their contributions and miss the point entirely. Our children are never "merely cute." They are taking their place in deeply and profoundly telling the glorious story of salvation.[9]

As it stands, the lack of true intentionality in integrating all generations present into the worship life of the church relegates everyone's involvement to simply worshiping in the same room at the same time.

A Possible Remedy

Is this the end? Have we lost the opportunity to worship intergenerationally forever? The answer is a resounding no! What then are church leaders to do to fix the problem? Whenever questions of how best to lead in ministry or worship arise, the foundational answers can always be found within the

---

9. Vanderwell, *Church of All Ages*, 183.

Introduction

pages of God's Word. Though the words *intergenerational worship* cannot be found in Scripture, the concept of one generation guiding and instructing others in worship is plentiful. Part one of this book will delve into what Scripture has to say about intergenerational worship—God's commands and man's attempts to fulfill those commands. God established the patterns for worship in the creation narrative in Genesis. It is here that the Creator also provided for the institution of the family. From the outset we see God's mandate to be fruitful and multiply applied to the life of the family and eventually the church. I believe that fruitful living can be summed up in two words: making disciples. As the biblical narrative continues, the mandate to make disciples is further enriched in the liturgy of the Passover, in Deuteronomy, and within the text of the Psalms. The New Testament further refines the nature of worship in the disciple-making process. Throughout the Scriptures, we can find an encouragement or even, dare I say, the command to be intergenerational in the way that we approach our weekly worship gatherings.

Once we have a firm grasp on what the Bible teaches about worshiping intergenerationally, part two will then seek to define ways to apply biblical intergenerational worship principles in the modern church. We will closely examine the role of being intentional in the worship planning and leading process and how it will help to engender true intergenerationality. To do so, I will suggest the concept of intentional mutuality—the purposefully designed reciprocal interaction of multiple generations in worship. I will make the argument that a foundational principle for transitioning a church from simple multigenerationality to true intergenerationality is implementing intentional mutuality within the context of the church's worship life. Part three will then offer specific ideas and resources for incorporating intentional mutuality in worship.

It is my hope that as you read through the text to follow, you will be convicted to take a hard look at the way you are currently "doing" church. Ask yourself the following questions:

Questions for Thought and Discussion

1. How do our current ministries align with what Ps 145 admonishes us to do?

2. Are the generations in our churches commending God's character, nature, and works to other generations?

3. Are we taking the easy road and delegating the worship discipleship of succeeding generations to the professionals in children's church and other age-segregated worship services?

4. Are we seeking comfort in worshiping with those who are just like us?

5. Are we taking the difficult steps to be intentional as we seek to involve all generations in worship and worship leadership.

PART ONE

What Does the Bible Say About Intergenerational Worship?

> All Scripture is breathed out by God and profitable for teaching, for reproof, for correction, and for training in righteousness, that the man of God may be complete, equipped for every good work.
>
> 2 TIMOTHY 3:16–17

As I think back throughout my life, I remember some incredible gifts that I've received. I remember the time my parents were in seminary, and they wanted to give me something special but really didn't have the money to do so. So, they found a bicycle that someone had thrown away. They lovingly sanded it, painted it, replaced all the damaged bits, and I found it under the tree on Christmas morning. I didn't know the story behind the bicycle until years later as an adult. All I knew at the time was how excited I was to have my very own bike.

God has also given us an incredible gift in the pages of his word. He has given us not only a blueprint for living but a narrative of his love for us and the entire world. Within its pages, God has woven together a tapestry that is more intricate and beautiful than anything we could ever imagine. This past February, I was able to tour the Biltmore Estate in Asheville, North Carolina, for the first time. While the whole building was awe inspiring, the one room that still stands out in my memory is the tapestry room. There,

What Does the Bible Say About Intergenerational Worship?

visitors can view several tapestries that were woven in Flanders back in the mid-sixteenth century. The skill and intricacy with which the weavers practiced their art still conjures the imagination to dream almost half a millennium later. I can also imagine that if I were to return today, I would see details that I missed the first time. Even though the metaphor pales in comparison to the overwhelming message of God's word, we can still understand that while there is great beauty and artistry in the Biltmore tapestries, there is an even greater artistry, purpose, and meaning behind every verse and every chapter in Scripture. God has granted us access to what some have called, not history, but "His-Story."

Think about it this way. There is an arc to the pages of Scripture. Everything that God has included is there for a reason. The Old Testament is not just a collection of stories that we read to Sunday school children; its narratives all point to the coming of the Messiah. And as we move to the New Testament, God fulfills those promises as he reveals himself in a physical way through Jesus Christ. Wow! We have access to God's playbook for all human history, and that arc of the gospel has some incredible implications as we seek to learn about God's plan for his people in worship.

In the next three chapters, we will delve into passages that deal with intergenerational worship concepts. But while we may focus on individual passages, don't forget that each verse is part of that arc of the gospel; they are all a part of His-Story. As we begin to comprehend God's original plan for us in worship, we will probably start to see that maybe what we're doing now might not truly measure up to his standard. That measuring stick is one of the best and worst aspects of Scripture, it reveals just how far off God's intended trajectory we've wandered.

I received a call from my wife shortly after purchasing our first GPS unit—this was back before it was on our smart phones. She was traveling out of town and had programed her destination into the unit. As she drove, she began to follow its instructions. It led her down some different roads than she had ever been on before. I still remember the call I received from her. She had no clue where she was and didn't know how to get out of the situation in which she found herself. The conversation went something like this:

My wife: I am so lost.
Me: Just tell me where you are.
My wife: I have no clue where I am.
Me: Well, just describe what you see.

Introduction

My wife: I'm in the middle of a field . . . with the cows.

Just like in any journey, to be successful you must know two things: your starting point and your final destination. We had to backtrack to a point where we could figure out my wife's location and then plot a course that would lead her to where she had intended to go all along. God has called us to live and lead a certain way and we've all wound up in a field surrounded by cows. To get out of that field and away from those cows, we must first figure out where we departed God's set path. Once we know where we are, we must then fix our eyes firmly on the destination. Finally, once we're armed with all the knowledge we need, we will be able to navigate through all the twists and turns of life to get to where God has called us to go.

So, let's study God's road map and plot a course of worship that follows his directions. But as always, we must determine where the journey begins. So, let's start at the very beginning. For the purpose of our study, that is the moment God spoke the world into existence.

2

The Old Testament

WE HAD COME TO the final moments of my doctoral work. I had completed all my seminars and passed all my written exams. The only obstacle that stood between me and starting my dissertation was an oral qualifying examination. I had prepared as much as I could for this multi-hour, intense question-and-answer session. The day arrived and we spent a good amount of time covering the basics. Then it was time for some specific questions about worship. One of the faculty members asked me to list some Scriptures that I felt were significant in the study of worship. I immediately responded with Gen 1:1 and following. At that moment, the professor asking the question shouted "YES," stopped me, and said—with a twinkle in his eye—that we could just end the questions at that point. What was the reason for his excitement? So many times, as we focus on worship, we immediately turn to Exod 24 (the first corporate worship service in the Bible), Isa 6 (a biblical model for worship), or even John 4 (the seminal moment when Jesus moves worship from the realm of physicality to the realm of spirituality). However, we don't often return to the garden of Eden. We simply gloss over the events of creation to "get to the good stuff," all the while not realizing that our learning about worship really starts in Gen 1:1, "In the beginning, God . . ." Within the events surrounding creation, God sets the pattern for all the worship that is to come for the rest of time.

Author and biblical scholar Allen Ross has stated that the end goal of creation and subsequent redemption was communion with God, and that our communion together should lie at the very heart of our worship.[10] The

---

10. Ross, *Recalling the Hope of Glory*, 82.

The Old Testament

Scriptures are explicit, God created man to live in a communal relationship with him. God didn't just create mankind and then leave them to fend for themselves. It was not like the old pervasive infomercial slogan of set it and forget it! God walked and talked with his creation in the cool of the garden (Gen 3:8). He desired an intimate relationship with them. But God didn't just stop there—no, he wanted that communal relationship to extend even further.

When God created humankind, he also created us within the context of community. He could have fashioned Adam from the dust, said that was very good, and spent eternity fellowshipping with his sole human creation. But God didn't stop with Adam. When he created man, he also created someone to complement Adam—Eve. In doing so, God formulated the building block of society: the family. He also established the foundational way of worship: Adam and Eve together, worshiping God in community. In those moments, God also gave mankind an example of community.

The concept of worshiping in the context of a community has some deep theological implications. Scottish theologian James B. Torrance finds the ultimate realization of worshiping in community within the communion of the Trinity. Torrance contends that when we worship, we participate in the communion among the Trinity through the Spirit.[11] We can experience communion with God through the Holy Spirit, participating in the sacrifice of the Son. While we worship in and through the Trinity, that example extends to our human community and especially our families.

God's design at creation included a dominion mandate for the family to be fruitful and multiply. In Gen 1:28, God commands, "Be fruitful and multiply and fill the earth and subdue it." In discussing the mandate, professor and reformed theologian John Frame states,

> It is appropriate that the hearing of these words be presented in Scripture as man's first experience. For this was the experience by which the whole course of man's life was determined. When man heard these words of God, he heard God's own definition of man. God was telling man who man was, what his task was. Everything else that man did was to be in obedience to this command. Whether a shepherd, a farmer, a miner, a businessman, a teacher, or a homemaker, his main job was to replenish and subdue the earth in obedience to this command. The command covered *all* of life, not just some compartments of it.[12]

---

11. Torrance, *Worship, Community, Triune God*, 15.
12. Frame, *History of Western Philosophy*, 639.

What Does the Bible Say About Intergenerational Worship?

As Frame alludes, the mandate of Gen 1:28 has often been interpreted to reveal only man's responsibility to procreate and subdue the earth. However, Frame has widened that perspective, encompassing the entirety of man's life in the enormity of God's command. Voddie Baucham adapts Frame's perspective to include spiritual mentoring within the family. Baucham states that "we see in the dominion mandate the absolute necessity of the practice of family discipleship."[13] Much like Baucham, authors George Willard Cochran Jr. and Brian C. Richardson also contend that God's command to subdue and rule "included exercising godly leadership within the family."[14] Leading the family in a godly way is, at its heart, spiritual formation. As will be seen in passages discussed in the following pages, fathers have been given the responsibility for leading their families.[15] The godly leadership fathers are to exert is modeled when God commands to Adam to work and keep the garden (Gen 2:15). As will be discussed later, Adam's working and keeping are more than physical labors—there is a spiritual counterpart to his physical effort.

In the discussions of the biblical texts that follow, God's command in Gen 1:28 will presuppose the physicality of procreation and subjection. However, expounding on concepts introduced by Frame, Baucham, Cochran, and Richardson, the dominion mandate will be further spiritually applied to our spiritual communities—both the family and the church. We can best sum up the spiritual nature of the dominion mandate in the words of Christ: "Go, therefore, and make disciples" (Matt 28:19). The family's command to make disciples begins with their biological children and continues as each generation in turn imparts knowledge of God's nature and ways to successive generations. Likewise, for the church, making disciples includes equipping and aiding in the spiritual formation of every participant in every generation. As we will see, all of this is closely tied to the way we worship together. Whether gathered around the table at home or with hundreds of other believers in church, God has called us to make disciples. That mandate has vast implications in the way we are to worship. Let's begin by closely examining how God introduced mankind to worship within the confines of the garden.

---

13. Baucham, *Family Shepherds*, 21.
14. Cochran and Richardson, "Why Your Child's Brain," 213.
15. See Deut 4:9–10; 6:1–9; 11:18–19; 32:45–47; and Ps 78:5.

The Old Testament

WORSHIP IN THE GARDEN

The narrative of creation and the garden is rich in symbolism that relates to all creation worshiping God. Allen Ross tells us that the revelation of God in creation is foundational to worship because it reveals that God is Sovereign as expressly seen in his work of creation and redemption.[16] God established a pattern of interaction with man at creation—God revealed himself and man responded. This key concept of worship initiation is of utmost importance throughout the remainder of human history. God sought out Adam and Eve for fellowship with him—they had direct access to God (Gen 1:28–40). According to Ross, communion with God is the goal of both creation and redemption, and the nature of communion is relational.[17] Communion, according to the dictionary, is intimate fellowship.[18] From the outset, God revealing himself and man's relational response sets the pattern for worship that can be found throughout the remainder of Scripture.

There are distinct ties between the garden of Eden and God's design, or pattern for worship. Gregory Beale, biblical scholar and professor at Reformed Theological Seminary, offers several observations proposing the garden was the first sanctuary.[19] First, man walked and talked with the Creator in the garden. The close communion between creation and Creator indicates that the garden was a place where man had immediate access to God. Second, Adam was commissioned by God to conform to a priestly role. In Gen 2:15 God tells Adam that he is to both work and keep the garden. The Hebrew terms used to describe Adam's work, *'āvad* (work) and *shāmar* (keep), are the same terms used to describe the worship work of the Levites in the temple (see Num 4:23–24). God's command to Adam to work and keep the garden are also closely aligned with the dominion mandate in Gen 1:28. Beale contends that the two functions of Adam expressed in Gen 2:15 should have ultimately culminated in Adam and his descendants expanding the borders of the garden until it encompassed the whole of the earth.[20] However, the completion of his task was interrupted by man's sin and its resulting consequence: loss of intimate communion with God through banishment from the garden. Because of Adam's sin, God expelled

---

16. Ross, *Recalling the Hope of Glory*, 78–81.
17. Ross, *Recalling the Hope of Glory*, 82.
18. Merriam-Webster, "Communion."
19. Beale, "Eden, Temple, Church's Mission," 7–10.
20. Beale, "Eden, Temple, Church's Mission," 10–11.

him from the garden and his priestly function was lost. Adam's role transformed from the Levitical tasks of working and keeping what God had entrusted to his care, to toiling in the soil just so that he might have food to eat (Gen 3:17–19). Other correlations of the garden and the temple, according to Beale, include: similarities in the tree of life and the golden lampstand,[21] the position of the garden and the temple as both were on a mountain and eastward facing,[22] the tree of knowledge echoing the ark of the covenant containing God's law,[23] and references in Ezek 28:13–19 calling Eden the holy mountain of God.[24] Beale concludes that the garden and the later temples were simply allusions to God's true eternal sanctuary—much like an architectural model points to a finished structure.[25]

The garden was God's initial revelation of the pattern of worship for his people that would be seen throughout the remainder of Scripture—God revealed himself and man responded. God issued a commission and man responded by working and keeping. The revelation and response pattern God designed also allowed for true communion between Creator and creation. In the garden man was able to freely commune with God. God revealed himself to Adam and Eve, and they responded to God's revelation. At its essence, God's act of creation set the pattern of revelation and response for all worship to follow. The relational nature found in God's revelation/response worship design lies at the heart of intergenerational worship and ministry. As a part of God's relational design, he also instituted the family at creation.

THE FAMILY AND THE DOMINION MANDATE

> Then the man said, "This at last is bone of my bones and flesh of my flesh; she shall be called Woman, because she was taken out of Man." Therefore, a man shall leave his father and his mother and hold fast to his wife, and they shall become one flesh. (Gen 2:23–24)

---

21. Beale, "Eden, Temple, Church's Mission," 10–11.
22. Beale, "Eden, Temple, Church's Mission," 10–11.
23. Beale, "Eden, Temple, Church's Mission," 10–11.
24. Beale, "Eden, Temple, Church's Mission," 10.
25. Beale, "Eden, Temple, Church's Mission," 18.

> And God blessed them. And God said to them, "Be fruitful and multiply and fill the earth and subdue it, and have dominion over the fish of the sea and over the birds of the heavens and over every living thing that moves on the earth." (Gen 1:28)

The family was the first institution created by God in Genesis. The family then becomes the major societal building block in Israel and eventually the New Testament church. God first created man and gave him dominion over the earth (Gen 1:26–28). In all of God's creation, at every step, God declared his work in creation as good (see Gen 1:10, 12, 18, 21, 25, and 31), yet as man began to exert his dominion over creation, God declared that it was not good for man to be alone (Gen 2:18). Therefore, he took a rib from Adam and created a helper, a partner in the work God had called man to do. God declared that the man and wife shall become one flesh (Gen 2:24) and work together. In that moment, God created and instituted the family. It is on this primary building block that society is formed. In every age since, God has used the family to both fill the earth and spiritually form their children and their children's children.

God has given the family a simple mandate: to be fruitful and multiply (Gen 1:28). As discussed earlier, the simplicity of being fruitful and multiplying has two primary connotations that have deeper implications. First, God has called the family to procreate, to physically multiply. God created man and woman uniquely to propagate the human race. It is only through the proper union of man and woman that children are born and the family is expanded. Second, God has mandated that the family be fruitful. As demonstrated earlier, Frame, Baucham, Cochran, and Richardson all indicate that being fruitful is more than physical procreation—there is a spiritual element as well.[26] God has given the man and woman charge over the spiritual, emotional, and physical development of the family by commanding them to be fruitful. They are to ensure that all family members grow in the knowledge and understanding of living by God's design. Regarding God's mandate to be fruitful and multiply, family ministry pioneer Diana Garland further contends that men and women are created to be on mission together—to minister to and with the family.[27] To fulfill God's command, parents must become spiritual catalysts for their children. The mandate to be fruitful and multiply can be summarized in one act: to make

---

26. See Frame, *History of Western Philosophy*, 639; Baucham, *Family Shepherds*, 21; and Cochran and Richardson, "Why Your Child's Brain," 213.

27. Garland, *Family Ministry*, 138.

disciples. God instituted the family to make disciples, and I believe this mandate foreshadows the purpose of the church in future years.

GOD FORMS COVENANTAL RELATIONSHIPS WITH HIS CREATION

Noah

> Then God said to Noah and to his sons with him, "Behold, I establish my covenant with you and your offspring after you." (Gen 9:8–9)

As the world continued to stray farther from God's intended plan of communion, God destroyed all of mankind through a flood. In essence, God created a living picture of his creative and redemptive power. Following the flood, God entered into covenant with Noah and his descendants, which begins a theme of covenantal relationship that will follow throughout the course of Scripture. While normally viewed as the institution of human government, the dominion mandate reiterated in Gen 9:1 and again in 9:7 offers some connection to Gen 1:28. God continues to extend his mandate for making disciples through his covenant with Noah. According to Robert Webber, a covenant is a treaty for "maintaining relationships without the use of force."[28] Covenants, prevalent in the political realm of the ancient world, were never used in the pagan's relationship with their god(s).[29] However, God began to employ covenants with his chosen people so that he might be able to define and regulate their worship practices.[30]

A significant part of God's covenants include an element of promise. In the Noahic covenant, God promises that he will never again bring destruction to the earth in the form of a flood. More than a promise, there is also a sense of commission included in this covenant. God reiterates the mandate given to Adam and Eve in the garden by telling Noah to "be fruitful and multiply, increase greatly on the earth and multiply in it" (Gen 9:7). The covenant God made with Noah was to extend to his offspring and to all the generations to come. The heritage of faith passed on from Noah to his descendants still reverberates in the faithful today. The Noahic covenant

---

28. Webber, *Biblical Foundations of Christian Worship*, 56.
29. Webber, *Biblical Foundations of Christian Worship*, 56.
30. Webber, *Biblical Foundations of Christian Worship*, 56.

displays the importance of looking toward future generations in God's redemptive plan.[31]

Abraham

> And I will establish my covenant between me and you and your offspring after you throughout their generations for an everlasting covenant, to be God to you and to your offspring after you. (Gen 17:7)

Following the Noahic covenant, Abraham also entered into a covenant relationship with God beginning in Gen 15. God proclaimed that Abraham's offspring would be as numerous as the stars in the heaven (Gen 15:5), and that they would inherit the land of Canaan (Gen 15:18). As God continued to work in the life of Abraham, God found him to be faithful. His initial call to Abraham was to *go* and *be*: to leave the land of his forefathers and to live righteously.[32] As a result of Abraham's faithfulness, God blessed him and honored the covenant by making him the father of the nation of Israel.

An important aspect regarding the covenant between God and Abraham is its generational focus. The covenant passed from one generation to the next. For this to occur, the previous generation must lead and instruct succeeding generations in the life of faith. At this point in history there was no organized religious training. The instruction of the young fell to the parents, namely the fathers, to see that their offspring remained faithful to the shared covenant. The Abrahamic covenant was sealed as Abraham set his heart to follow after God.[33]

Succeeding Generations

> And in your offspring shall all the nations of the earth be blessed, because you have obeyed my voice. (Gen 22:18)

In the Abrahamic covenant God proclaimed that the descendants of Abraham would be as numerous as the stars in the heavens (Gen 15:5). But as Abraham and his wife Sarah were entering into old age without an heir, the promise of God appeared to be impossible. Abraham wrestled with the

---

31. Pendergraft, "Credobaptist Defense," 46.
32. Ross, *Recalling the Hope of Glory*, 135.
33. Schultz, *Old Testament Speaks*, 34.

What Does the Bible Say About Intergenerational Worship?

inability to conceive with Sarah and sought to bring about the fulfillment of God's covenant through his own actions with Hagar. Nonetheless, God realized the covenant through the birth of Isaac. Abraham taught Isaac regarding faith in God.[34] God then called to Abraham and tested him. God required the sacrifice of Isaac as an act of faith. Although in Abraham's estimation this would interrupt God's promise of blessing future generations through him, Abraham complied and willingly prepared the sacrifice. God intervened and provided a suitable sacrifice instead. As a result of Abraham's faithfulness God sealed his covenant with Abraham and his descendants: "I will surely bless you, and I will surely multiply your offspring as the stars of heaven and as the sand that is on the seashore . . . because you have obeyed my voice" (Gen 22:17–18).

Robert Pendergraft, professor of worship at the University of Mary Hardin-Baylor, suggests that although these covenantal passages in Genesis point toward future generations, one must not infer that all children of the covenant are assured salvation.[35] While faith is to be passed from one generation to the next, it must be actively taught to and accepted by future generations. Salvation cannot be assumed by simple heritage; it is received through faith in Christ alone (Rom 10:9–10). God has indicated through these covenantal passages that future generations are important and that they must be brought to maturity with an understanding of the salvific nature of Christ's sacrifice.

Generations in the Passover

> And when your children say to you, "What do you mean by this service?" you shall say, "It is the sacrifice of the LORD's Passover, for he passed over the houses of the people of Israel in Egypt, when he struck the Egyptians but spared our houses." (Exod 12:26–27)

---

34. In Gen 18:19 God says of Abraham, "For I have chosen him, that he may command his children and his household after him to keep the way of the Lord by doing righteousness and justice, so that the Lord may bring to Abraham what he has promised him." In Gen 21:4, Abraham circumcises Isaac thereby bringing him into the covenantal relationship with God. Later, as Abraham was commissioned by God to sacrifice his son, Isaac showed knowledge of sacrificial worship when he questioned his father as to the whereabouts of the sacrifice. "And Isaac said to his father Abraham, 'Behold, the fire and the wood, but where is the lamb for a burnt offering?'" (Gen 22:7).

35. Pendergraft, "Credobaptist Defense," 47.

The Old Testament

As we move forward in time, the children of Israel have slipped away from worshiping God. As a result, God allows his people to be placed into slavery in Egypt. The Hebrews remain in Egypt for four hundred years, all the while calling out for salvation. God hears their prayer and raises up Moses to deliver his people from the hand of Pharaoh. Through incredible miracles and signs, Pharaoh is finally convinced to release the people. Once free, God's people continue to see his hand at work as the Red Sea is parted and Pharaoh's army—the mightiest in the world—is swallowed up and destroyed.

To commemorate the events surrounding the exodus, God institutes the Passover celebration. Passover is a prime exemplar of worship in an intergenerational context. According to Scott Brown, the Passover's purpose was to "inspire belief in one's sons and sons' sons."[36] The concept of retelling the works of God in the presence or hearing of sons and grandsons harkens back to the plagues in Egypt when God told Moses to "tell in the hearing of your son and of your grandson how I have dealt harshly with the Egyptians and what signs I have done among them, that you may know that I am the Lord" (Exod 10:2).

At Passover, the whole family is to be present for the celebration. In the midst of the celebration, the children are to ask, "What do you mean by this service?" (Exod 12:26). In other words, the children have a specific role to play in the drama of the Passover worship. While they participate, they also can learn and be spiritually formed by what they see, hear, and do. Duane Garrett states that Passover, like other feasts and festivals, is a "teaching aid designed to prompt the curiosity of children."[37] In other words, the children are present and are integrally involved in the service of worship surrounding Passover. Matthew Henry says that "it is a good thing to see children inquisitive about the things of God; it is to be hoped that those who are careful to ask for the way will find it."[38] The relevant issue is that all generations are present, participating, and interacting with one another. The annual celebration of the Passover affords fathers the opportunity to commend God's works to the next generation and involve them in worship. It also allows the emerging generations to see God's power modeled, God's provision celebrated, and God's name and character exalted. These experiences both spiritually form the next generation and also prepare them to understand that they have a place and a role in worship among God's

---

36. Brown, *A Weed in the Church*, 95.
37. Garrett, *Commentary on Exodus*, 364.
38. Henry, *Genesis to Deuteronomy*, 253.

people because it is finally time to see the ultimate result of the exodus—communal worship.

God's People in Worship—Together!

> Then he took the Book of the Covenant and read it in the hearing of the people. And they said, "All that the Lord has spoken we will do, and we will be obedient." (Exod 24:7)

The primary focus of the exodus from Egypt was not freedom for the children of Israel. God wanted his people free so that they could worship him. Think back to Moses's interactions with Pharaoh. Each time Moses asked Pharaoh to let God's people go, the reason he gave was so that they might move into the wilderness to worship God. All of the plagues, the flight from Egypt, the passage through the Red Sea, the destruction of the Egyptian army were all leading to this specific point in time.

Exodus 24 stands as a seminal passage in the study of Old Testament worship. At the base of Mt. Sinai, the people of God are finally able to express themselves in worship—together! It is in these moments that God initiates the pattern for worship that would be in use throughout the remainder of the Old Testament and beyond. The dialogical nature of worship that is found in these verses exemplifies the nature of the communion God has with his people—God reveals himself and the people respond in worship.[39]

In previous texts, God encouraged the participation of emerging generations in worship. As Noah and his family emerged from the ark, they built an altar and worshiped God together. During the Passover celebration, children were actively involved in the ceremony. One can likewise assume that when the Scripture states that *all* the people of God gathered at Mt. Sinai to worship, children, young people, and adults were all included.[40]

---

39. The revelation/response pattern of worship is evident throughout the Old Testament. It is found in the garden of Eden, is later expounded upon by the prophet Isaiah (Isa 6) and is woven throughout the remainder of Scripture. As God reveals himself, the people respond. The six-fold structure of worship found in Exod 24 becomes the pattern for worship in the remainder of the Old Testament. (1) God reveals himself and calls the people to worship, (2) the people acknowledge and confess their need for forgiveness, (3) God provides atonement, (4) God speaks his word, (5) the people respond with commitment, and (6) God hosts a celebratory feast.

40. Exod 24:3 states that "Moses came and told the people all the words of the Lord and all the rules. And *all* the people answered with one voice" (emphasis added).

The Old Testament

As the people of God responded to the revelations of God through worship, all the generations of the people observed and participated. Exodus 24:5 states Moses selected some young men to help lead the people in worship. Duane Garrett contends that Moses using *young* men was both practical and symbolic because the young men represented Israel's future.[41] Every generation experienced the revelation of God through the proclamations and reading. Likewise, every generation then responded by proclaiming their obedience to God's law (Exod 19:8, 24:7). When the thunder roared and lightning flashed while Moses met with God on the mountain, all the people witnessed the power of God from the camp (Exod 19:17, 20:18). One can also imagine that God's demonstrations initiated teaching times from parent to child as the children questioned the displays of God's power and heard God's law proclaimed (Exod 24:3).

As worship became more and more formalized around the tabernacle in the wilderness, God continued to reveal more of his plan for worshiping together. Continuing through the Pentateuch, Moses gives the children of God specific instructions relating to incorporating all the generations in worship—beginning with parental involvement in the spiritual development of their children. In Deut 4, 6, and 11, God commands parents to teach the things of God to their children.

Parents, Teach Your Children!

> Only take care, and keep your soul diligently, lest you forget the things that your eyes have seen, and lest they depart from your heart all the days of your life. Make them known to your children and your children's children. (Deut 4:9)

Some of my family was traveling in the car yesterday, coming home from lunch after our Sunday morning service. The radio was on in the background, and as my wife and twenty-year-old daughter—home from college over spring break—were talking, a familiar song began to play. We all began to sing to Whitney Houston's song "Greatest Love of All," where she begins by declaring that children are important to the future and so we should instruct them and love them.[42] The first few words have always struck a chord in me. While I do not agree with the theology of this particular pop song, the message is one that reminds us of an important truth about the necessity

---

41. Garrett, *Commentary on Exodus*, 543.
42. Houston, "Greatest Love of All."

What Does the Bible Say About Intergenerational Worship?

of mentoring the next generation. Even the secular world understands that children need to be taught well so that they might one day be ready to lead. But God had already put a plan into motion thousands of years ago.

As we look closely at the arc of worship in Scripture, we begin to see God's plan take shape. God institutes the tabernacle, and the people finally have a focal point for gathering together in worship. Even more, though, God is preparing his people to make disciples. As the generation who saw God's mighty hand at work in the exodus begins to die, God has a plan for those coming after to know and understand their relationship with him.

Deuteronomy 4:9–10 begins a series of three passages that encourage intergenerational mentoring among God's people. Each one exhorts parents to teach the ways, works, knowledge, and fear of God to their children and later generations. The children of Israel had seen marvelous things. They had experienced the angel of death passing over their homes. They had seen a pursuing army swallowed up by the Red Sea. They had seen God provide for their every physical need. They had also seen God move in other miraculous ways as they continued to traverse through the wilderness. So that current and future generations might not forget what God had done, God instructed parents to recount his mighty acts to their children. Duane Christensen contends that "the future of Israel is dependent on the transmission of the experience of God's mighty acts in history, and his demands, to each successive generation."[43] Again, the onus is on the parent to relate to successive generations what God has done.

Except at rare times, the Old Testament father would be the only priest that the children would ever see. In Gen 8:20 and Gen 12:7–8, both Noah and Abraham led their families in worship and offered sacrifices as they built altars to the Lord.[44] Harkening back to Adam's priestly roles of working and keeping, and as exemplified by Noah and Abraham, fathers performed the rites that would later become the responsibility of the priests of the tabernacle and the temple. In much the same way, following the birth of Isaac, Abraham performed the rite of circumcision.[45] In later generations,

---

43. Christensen, *Deuteronomy 1–11*, 80.

44. "Then Noah built an altar to the Lord and took some of every clean animal and some of every clean bird and offered burnt offerings on the altar" (Gen 8:20). "Then the Lord appeared to Abram and said, 'To your offspring I will give this land.' So he built there an altar to the Lord, who had appeared to him" (Gen 12:7).

45. "And Abraham circumcised his son Isaac when he was eight days old, as God had commanded him" (Gen 21:4).

fathers led their families in worship, most notably through the Passover meal.

Even after the construction of the temple in Jerusalem, the father was still the priest with whom the children would interact on a day-to-day basis. Families only traveled to the temple for special occasions. Michael and Michelle Anthony posit that the father's priestly role was one of education with an inherent dual purpose or intent.[46] First, the father was to impart the history of God's covenant with man and the ways in which God continued to honor that covenant. Second, the father was to instruct the children in ethical living—what it means to live a life of integrity and purpose within God's covenant. The two-fold focus of godly education was deeply impressed in Deut 4:9–10, but it is no more evident than in Deut 6.

The Shema

> And these words that I command you today shall be on your heart. You shall teach them diligently to your children, and shall talk of them when you sit in your house, and when you walk by the way, and when you lie down, and when you rise. (Deut 6:6–7)

Known as the Shema from the opening word of Deut 6:4, this passage encapsulates the worship of God for the Israelite people: "Hear, O Israel: The LORD our God, the LORD is one. You shall love the LORD your God with all your heart and with all your soul and with all your might" (Deut 6:4–5). The command in Deut 6:5 is to love God completely and singularly. The three adverbial clauses—with all your heart, soul, and might—should not be seen, according to Malcolm Yarnell, as singular acts of worship but as an "absolute singularity of personal devotion to God."[47] Yet, the singularity of devotion is directed toward the plurality of a relational Triune God. The Shema indicates that the "Lord, *our* God, the Lord is one" (Deut 6:4; emphasis added). God is "our" God. His desire is that a deep, abiding relationship will develop between Creator and creation. For that relationship to grow, each party must be known by the other. God revealed himself and his character to Moses through his name (YHWH—I AM WHO I AM) in Exod 3:14, and his command is to worship. Yarnell further contends that "to worship God truly is to engage the unified life of the Father, the Son,

---

46. Anthony and Anthony, *Theology for Family Ministries*, 25.
47. Yarnell, *God the Trinity*, 76.

What Does the Bible Say About Intergenerational Worship?

and the Holy Spirit . . . worshiping the one God alone."[48] The emphasis of worship in the Shema became the root of the law of God's children. Faithful Jews to this day quote the words of Deut 6:4–7 every morning and evening.

Emphasis can also be found in the relationality of how the law is to be taught. The summation of the law found in this passage is to be taught *diligently* (Deut 6:7). Moses places great importance on the transmission of God's commands from one generation to the next. The ways of God should be the subject of conversations throughout the daily life of the family. They should be written on the doorposts of the home so that each time the family passes through the portal they are reminded of the might of God. They should be as close as the hand and the forehead. For successful transmission, the fear and knowledge of God must be placed in their hearts and passed on to their children's children. To do so, Moses gives specific examples of how God's truth should be transmitted to successive generations.

The nature, character, and ways of God are to be taught when sitting at home, when walking, when going to sleep, and when the family awakens in the morning. Moses is specific—God's people are to always practice the art of mentoring with successive generations, so that the mysteries and majesties of God would be understood, respected, and remembered. The father is a key figure in this mentoring process. As mentioned earlier, the father was the priestly figure of the home, and it was his God-given responsibility to impart the expectations and rewards of covenantal relationship to successive generations. These same thoughts conclude in Deut 11:18–19:

> You shall therefore lay up these words of mine in your heart and in your soul, and you shall bind them as a sign on your hand; and they shall be as frontlets between your eyes. You shall teach them to your children, talking of them when you are sitting in your house, and when you are walking by the way, and when you lie down, and when you rise.

In this text, God outlines his instructions to parents and other mature adults to disciple those who are immature in the knowledge and ways of God. The passages encourage parents to take advantage of teachable moments. Matthew Henry suggests three rules that are found in this passage. First, man is to fill his heart with the word of God. Second, man's eyes are to be fixed on God's word. Third, man should use his tongue to speak about the word of God.[49] Henry says that speaking God's word is especially im-

---

48. Yarnell, *God the Trinity*, 57.
49. Henry, *Genesis to Deuteronomy*, 602.

portant when relating to children. He states that children "must be taught the service of God as the one thing needful, much more needful than either the rules of decency or the calling they must live by in this world."[50] As the primary disciple maker, the parent is responsible for the spiritual instruction of their children.

I hope that you are beginning to see the necessity for adults to come alongside emerging generations to impart the knowledge of God to them. God has called parents, first and foremost, to spiritually disciple their children. He also calls other adults to join with the parents in teaching and modeling the Christian life. As our focus now shifts away from the home and onto the gathered body of believers, please notice that the command still remains: we are called to make disciples.

TEACH THEM ABOUT GOD'S WRATH, TOO

> Hear of this, you elders; give ear, all inhabitants of the land! Has such a thing happened in your days, or in the days of your fathers? Tell your children of it, and let your children tell their children, and their children to another generation. (Joel 1:2–3)

Michael B. Shepherd indicates that the role of the book of Joel is to give introduction to the theme of the day of the LORD.[51] The book of Joel gives form to the wrath of God for the children of Israel and for modern-day believers. As has been previously discussed, God commanded one generation to commend his works, nature, and character to succeeding generations. However, what is found in Joel indicates that God also instructs his people to transmit the nature of his wrath and judgment. Just as our children need to hear of God's love and his redemptive character, they also need to understand that God is a God of wrath. God detests sin. Joel teaches us that the children of Israel were to teach their children, and their children were to teach their children to understand and see the holiness of God as demonstrated by his righteous wrath. An understanding of the true nature of God's holiness cannot be fully understood if you only examine his mercy and love. Mercy and justice go hand in hand, and generations, especially those so far removed from the severe judgments of God as in modern society, must comprehend that God is both loving and wrathful.

---

50. Henry, *Genesis to Deuteronomy*, 602.
51. Shepherd, *Book of the Twelve*, 116.

What Does the Bible Say About Intergenerational Worship?

Who Is Called to Worship?

> And you shall rejoice before the LORD your God, you and your sons and your daughters, your male servants and your female servants, and the Levite that is within your towns, since he has no portion or inheritance with you. (Deut 12:12)

Beginning in Deut 12:7–12, we find a series of passages that outline in detail who is to be present as the people gather in worship. As God instructs his people on the practices of worship, he is very specific about who is to be in attendance during worship. Robert Pendergraft states that "this passage demonstrates that there is no generational, ethnic, or socioeconomic preference when coming to worship; all are welcome. No matter one's age or occupation, he or she is called to join the rest of the family in worship."[52] Everyone in the nation of Israel was called to worship and participate in the sacrifices, celebrations, and feasts.

Matthew Henry proclaims that the children are to rejoice before the Lord so that the religious services would be pleasurable and not a "drudgery."[53] This concept brings us to an important fact: the acclimation of children to the corporate worship of the church as a whole is crucial to their continued worship participation in later life. In a 2017 research survey conducted by LifeWay, researchers found that spiritual health increased in 41 percent of children who were connected to multiple adults at church who intentionally invested in them spiritually.[54] From the gathered data, the study extrapolates that the more involved the parents are in church and the more connections they make within the corporate body, the "more likely they are to have enhanced relationships with other adults who could serve as mentors and investors in the lives of their own kids."[55] As older generations pour into the lives of the younger generations, the less mature are strengthened and given a life-long vision of what the church could and should be in the life of the family. The reverse is also true. As older generations pour into the lives of succeeding generations, the younger participants also begin to encourage the older—intentionally integrating the generations in worship leads to cross-generational learning.[56] There is a

---

52. Pendergraft, "Credobaptist Defense," 69.
53. Henry, *Genesis to Deuteronomy*, 606.
54. Magruder, *Nothing Less*, 95.
55. Magruder, *Nothing Less*, 95.
56. Allen and Ross state that intergenerational worship opportunities allow older

reciprocal relationship expressed in these passages that we will explore further in chapter 7. We must understand that God's command for everyone in all households to rejoice and worship together is still relevant in today's culture.

Concerning Feasts and Special Celebrations

> And you shall rejoice before the LORD your God, you and your son and your daughter, your male servant and your female servant, the Levite who is within your towns, the sojourner, the fatherless, and the widow who are among you, at the place that the LORD your God will choose, to make his name dwell there. (Deut 16:11)

Much like Deut 12, chapter 16 delineates who is to be present during times of national celebration and worship. The Feast of Weeks and Feast of Booths are times when God's people recognize his works and join together to give him praise and honor. The Feast of Weeks occurs seven weeks following Passover and marks the culmination of the grain harvest and the conclusion of an anxious period of waiting to see if the harvest would sustain them throughout the remainder of the year.

The Feast of Booths celebrated the ending of the agricultural year in ancient Israel. A festival of seven days, Booths, or Tabernacles, was a time of great rejoicing for the people of Israel as they brought offerings before the Lord and celebrated his goodness and provision. While only the adult men in ancient Israel brought the offerings, these passages illuminate that the women and children were also integrally involved in the celebrations.

Moses specifically indicates that during these times of rejoicing before the Lord, "your son and your daughter" are to be present (Deut 16:11 and 16:14). God commanded all the people to participate in the celebrations—men, women, children, servants, widows, orphans, travelers—all people. However, the festivals included more than just rejoicing. As all the people participated, they learned more about the nature and character of God. The festivals were times when the provision of God and his nature and character were trumpeted and extolled. Children were allowed to see the offerings brought by their fathers. They could smell the emanations from the altar. They could listen to the prayers and the praises. They learned by watching

---

generations to "pour their accumulated wisdom and insight into those coming along behind them," and younger generations "can provide new purpose . . . and can refocus attention" for older generations. Allen and Ross, *Intergenerational Christian Formation*, 62.

and participating in these large-scale worship events. We will learn in the following pages that worship is both formational and transformational. As we worship and as we spend time in communion with God, the Spirit works in us, and we are changed.

Moses Passes the Torch to the Next Generation

> Assemble the people, men, women, and little ones, and the sojourner within your towns, that they may hear and learn to fear the LORD your God, and be careful to do all the words of this law. (Deut 31:12)

As his ministry and life came to an end, Moses was very particular to follow God's commands in instructing the children of Israel regarding God's law. Matthew Henry states that Moses was "not only entrusted to deliver it [the Law] to that generation, but to transmit it to the generations to come."[57] Every seventh year during the Festival of Booths, the children of Israel were to gather to hear the public reading of the Law of God. As the people gathered to hear the Law, the whole of God's people gathered. Deuteronomy 31:12 states that the entirety of the people assembled together—men, women, little ones, and travelers. The purpose of gathering was to hear the Law of God and in turn learn to fear God and follow his law.

God commissioned Moses to write a song for the people of Israel. The song is the culmination of all the teachings of Moses to the children of Israel. In it he once again reiterates the responsibility of one generation transmitting the knowledge of the ways and character of God to succeeding generations.

> Take to heart all the words by which I am warning you today, that you may command them to your children, that they may be careful to do all the words of this law. (Deut 32:46)

In his final words to the people before his death, Moses underscores that the people must commend the words of God's law to the children. Scott Brown states that the commending of the law from parent to child is the primary trust God has placed in the hands of parents.[58] This life mission to which God has called all parents is stated and restated multiple times by

---

57. Henry, *Genesis to Deuteronomy*, 668.
58. Brown, *A Weed in the Church*, 85.

Moses in Deuteronomy as has been previously discussed (Deut 4:19; 6:6–7; 11:18–19). Brown further contends that "God loves multi-generational faithfulness, the declaration of His glory from grandfather and father to grandson and son."[59] Scripture instructs that God is pleased when generations of parents, and particularly fathers, fulfill their mission of teaching the following generation.

While this mission is primarily in the hands of the parents, it is the church's responsibility to come alongside and help equip them for this important task. Brown states, "The church needs the family, but the family also needs the church."[60] As is seen below in Josh 8, God calls the whole people of Israel together to hear his word proclaimed. Grandfathers and grandmothers with parents and children of all the families of Israel were to listen to the Law together. There was both support and accountability in gathering together.

Joshua Continues in Moses's Footsteps

> There was not a word of all that Moses commanded that Joshua did not read before all the assembly of Israel, and the women, and the little ones, and the sojourners who lived among them. (Josh 8:35)

After the fall of Ai, Joshua assembled the whole of the children of Israel so that the Law might be read aloud. The acts of worship carried out by Joshua and the people of God were described twice in orders given earlier by Moses.[61] Moses commanded Joshua to gather the people so that the words of the Law of God might be read. This reading of the Law was to occur when the people passed over into the land that God had promised them.

Much like Moses's final words to God's people in Deut 31, all the people gathered together to hear the Law of God read as a public act of worship—men, women, little ones, and travelers among them. Matthew

---

59. Brown, *A Weed in the Church*, 93.
60. Brown, *A Weed in the Church*, 117.
61. The act of worship described in Josh 8 was prescribed by Moses on two occasions. In Deut 11:29–30 Moses states, "And when the Lord your God brings you into the land that you are entering to take possession of it, you shall set the blessing on Mount Gerizim and the curse on Mount Ebal." In Deut 27:2–3 Moses proclaims, "And on the day you cross over the Jordan to the land that the Lord your God is giving you, you shall set up large stones and plaster them with plaster. And you shall write on them all the words of this law, when you cross over to enter the land that the Lord your God is giving you."

What Does the Bible Say About Intergenerational Worship?

Henry contends that the whole nation of Israel was present to hear from God. He states,

> Every Israelite was present, even *the women and the little* ones that all might know and do their duty. Note, Masters of families should bring their wives and children with them to the solemn assemblies for religious worship. All that are capable of learning must come to be *taught out of the law*.[62]

It is interesting to note that all who are capable of learning are to come and be taught the law. Many times, we think that the youngest among us—those nine-, ten-, eleven-, or twelve-year-olds—do not have the stamina or attention span to comprehend what is happening in our services. When Joshua called the people together, it was to read the whole of the Law. This activity wasn't quick and it wasn't easy, but it was utterly worthwhile. The church today does not set a high enough standard for our children. We have slipped into the fallacy that our children can only concentrate for a few minutes and then they will be a disruption in the proceedings. I would strenuously disagree. I am constantly amazed by how much our children retain in a normal worship service. In fact, I daresay that our children may have better recall than most of the adults present for the same service. There are great rewards for children who are present to hear Scripture being read and exegeted with their families. As Joshua exemplifies, all generations need to be present as God's word is read. An element of transmission is incomplete when God's word is only read and studied in age-segregated ministry silos. We again see this same idea in Neh 8:2 as the remnant of Israel is gathered together to hear the Law being read:

> So Ezra the priest brought the Law before the assembly, both men and women and all who could understand what they heard, on the first day of the seventh month.

Nehemiah 8:1–3 describes the reading of the Law following the rebuilding of the wall around Jerusalem. Nehemiah states that men and women and *everyone who could understand* gathered together to hear Ezra read the Law. While opponents of intergenerational worship may use this passage to limit the access of young children to worship, we must realize that the whole community was involved. Marvin Breneman states that those in attendance "involved the entire community, including young people and children. . . . The Old Testament emphasizes that God's Word is

---

62. Henry, *Joshua to Esther*, 39.

to be known and used by all the people, not only the priests and leaders."[63] Children and young people were integrally involved in times of both corporate and family worship. To insist that they would be excluded from this significant time of hearing the Law of God read would be inconsistent with previous instances of biblical worship.

In *A Weed in the Church*, Scott Brown cites several reasons why this passage is not exclusionary for children and youth in the corporate worship of Israel. First, Brown describes the intergenerational nature of the meeting. He states that it was an "explicitly gender and age-integrated gathering."[64] The inclusivity of all who could hear and understand, according to Brown, far outweighs its exclusivity. Second, the language of the text does not call for certain age groups to be removed. Children and young people are assumed to be excluded by those advocating age-segregated worship practices, but neither is specifically prohibited. Finally, the only category of people who are expressly excluded from participating are those who cannot understand. Those who cannot understand could encompass very small children, but it could also include those adults who speak a different language. Brown suggests that there would be children and even adults who would not understand the Hebrew language and would thus be excluded.[65] Therefore, one can contend that children and young people were not prohibited from attendance.

Looking Beyond the Here and Now

> Let us now build an altar, not for burnt offering, nor for sacrifice, but to be a witness between us and you, and between our generations after us, that we do perform the service of the Lord in his presence with our burnt offerings and sacrifices and peace offerings, so your children will not say to our children in time to come, "You have no portion in the Lord." (Josh 22:26–27)

In the conquest of Canaan, the two-and-a-half tribes (Reuben, Gad, and Manasseh) fulfilled their promise to fight alongside the armies of God (see Num 22:28–33). Therefore, Joshua dismissed them to return to the lands east of the Jordan river that were promised to them by God. While traveling home, they built an altar to the Lord on the border of the Jordan. The

---

63. Breneman, *Ezra, Nehemiah, Esther*, 224.
64. Brown, *A Weed in the Church*, 136.
65. Brown, *A Weed in the Church*, 138.

remaining tribes of Israel took offense. They believed that Reuben, Gad, and Manasseh were attempting to circumvent God's requirement to worship only at Shiloh.

In Josh 22:21–29, the two-and-a-half tribes plead their case that the altar was built to serve as a bridge of remembrance. It was built with future generations in view. The altar was erected to remind the people of Gad, Reuben, and Manasseh of their allegiance and service to God. Being so far removed from the place of worship God had chosen—Shiloh—the builders were anxious that future generations would not stray from faithfulness to God. Their hope was also that the ten tribes would not reject future generations because of difficulties in traveling to Shiloh to participate in feasts and festivals. The terrain and the impassability of the Jordan at times could cause interruption in travel. They feared future generations would be alienated from worshiping. The focus of the tribal leaders was to ensure that the discipling of future generations would be primary in their thinking and their actions. The builders of the altar subscribed to the long view of how future generations should come to an understanding of the ways and nature of God.

What Happens When a Generation Fails to Follow God's Commands?

> And all that generation also were gathered to their fathers. And there arose another generation after them who did not know the Lord or the work that he had done for Israel. (Judg 2:10)

As can be seen in the story of Israel, the knowledge and fear of God can seemingly disappear in just a single generation. At the conclusion of Joshua, Scripture states that Joshua and the elders who outlived him feared and served the Lord.[66] These leaders were the generation who had seen God do miraculous things from the deliverance from Egypt to the provision of God's hand in the wilderness wanderings. They had experienced firsthand the awesome power of the Lord. Yet as Joshua's generation passed, Israel slipped into paganism. Judges 2:11–12 says that "the people of Israel

---

66. "After these things Joshua the son of Nun, the servant of the Lord, died, being 110 years old. And they buried him in his own inheritance at Timnath-serah, which is in the hill country of Ephraim, north of the mountain of Gaash. Israel served the Lord all the days of Joshua, and all the days of the elders who outlived Joshua and had known all the work that the Lord did for Israel" (Josh 24:29–31).

The Old Testament

did what was evil in the sight of the Lord and served the Baals. And they abandoned the Lord, the God of their fathers, who had brought them out of the land of Egypt. They went after other gods." Brian Haynes concludes, "It only takes one generation of parents to forsake their role as faith trainers for a culture passionate about God to turn from Him and embrace the gods, belief systems, and lifestyle of the pagan."[67] I believe that we are beginning to reap these same consequences. We are seeing a generation of children coming of age who were taught by example that almost anything could be more important than attending church. Their parents would skip church on a Sunday or Wednesday because of a baseball or softball game. Those children internalized their parents' priorities. Now, that same generation is beginning to have their own children. They are stepping away from church in droves because other activities hold more relevance or sway over them. Attending church for them is just not that important. Much like Joshua's time, many churches today remain only one generation away from obscurity.

If a generation only once removed from seeing God's hand at work can so quickly devolve into idol worship, how much more tenuous is the grip of those who are thousands of years removed? LifeWay Research conducted a study in 2018 finding that 66 percent of students who were very active in church and ministry during their high school years left the church in their college years (ages eighteen to twenty-two).[68] While this statistic may be shocking, God had already prescribed the remedy in Deuteronomy—one generation is to actively instruct succeeding generations in the ways of God.[69] It is through the intentional instruction passed from adult to the young that the fear of God is instilled and awakened in the next generation. According to Scripture, the connection between parent and child is of primary importance in the transmission of faith between generations.

In the current church culture, separation of parent and child wrought by age segregation has impacted the role of the parent in discipling their children. Michael and Michelle Anthony state that "the church often allowed parents to *abdicate* this role [spiritually nurturing their children] to her by creating structures that enabled mothers and fathers to outsource religious and spiritual training to the 'professionals.'"[70] The structures formed

---

67. Haynes, *Legacy Path*, 2.
68. Trueblood, *Within Reach*, 12.
69. Deut 4:9–10; 6:1–9; and 11:18–19.
70. Anthony and Anthony, *Theology for Family Ministries*, 182; emphasis added.

by age-segregated churches not only enable parents to relinquish their role, but also encourage it with the promise of polished production values that will hold the attention of both child and adolescent, giving the parent a much-needed respite for adult interaction. While times of refreshing may be important, the nurturing role a parent or other adult plays is crucial in the spiritual formation of our children and students. The nurturing role is no more evident than when viewed in relation to worship. I will contend that emerging generations[71] need to see their parents and grandparents worship—there is something vitally important transmitted from mature to immature worshipers in the corporate context.

Worship in Times of Crisis

> Meanwhile all Judah stood before the LORD, with their little ones, their wives, and their children. (2 Chr 20:13)

Near the end of the rule of Jehoshaphat in Judah, armies from Moab and Ammon assembled to destroy Judah. In these moments, Jehoshaphat called for a time of national fasting and assembly so that they might call out to God for aid in their troubles.[72] Jehoshaphat cried out to God for deliverance from this threat (2 Chr 20:6–12). Jehoshaphat did so in the presence of the whole of Judah. In 2 Chr 20:13, the chronicler states that "all of Judah stood before the Lord, with *their little ones*, their wives, and *their children*" (emphasis added). At a moment of national crisis, all generations gathered together to seek out guidance from the Lord. Members of every generation saw others pleading before the Lord. In the end, God responded through Jahaziel who proclaimed that the battle belonged to the Lord and no one else (2 Chr 20:15). The armies of Judah had only to be faithful and take their place ready for battle. As they began to praise God, the Lord set an ambush for the armies of Moab and Ammon, and they were routed (2 Chr 20:22).

In much the same way, Joel chapter 2 begins with the sounding of an alarm—the blast of the shofar—to call all the people to repentance before the awful day of the LORD:

---

71. Strother uses the term *emerging generations* to encapsulate children and youth in any particular time period. Strother, "Family-Equipping Ministry," 145.

72. Merrill, *Commentary on 1 & 2 Chronicles*, 428.

> Blow the trumpet in Zion; consecrate a fast; call a solemn assembly; gather the people. Consecrate the congregation; assemble the elders, gather the children, even nursing infants. Let the bridegroom leave his room, and the bride her chamber. (Joel 2:15–16)

Joel, speaking of swarms of locusts that will devour the land, is describing attacking armies that will lay waste to the land if the people do not repent. The alarm is raised for all the people—no one is to be excluded. Joel calls the people to gather the elders, children, and even the infants. They are to be called to fasting and a solemn assembly. The purpose of the fasting and assembly is repentance. Joel proclaims that the people are to "rend your hearts and not your garments" (Joel 2:13). It is to be a focused time of introspection as the people of God seek him out and turn from the error of their ways as a nation.

What is most compelling in this narrative is the scope of the repentance. Joel calls all the people of every generation—infants to elders. While Joel 1:1–3 instructs God's people on the importance of teaching future generations about the righteous wrath of God, Joel 2 insists that God's people must also instruct future generations on the nature of repentance. There is an inherent intergenerational nature of worship described in Joel's text. Not only are the children to learn from the solemn assembly of the whole nation, but they in turn will also teach their parents. Joel is calling all the people to fast. As the infants are kept from feeding, the cries of hunger will help draw the parents to repentance. The interaction of the various generations described here is one aspect of true intergenerational worship—generations affecting spiritual growth in other generations.

Worship in Times of Celebration

> And they offered great sacrifices that day and rejoiced, for God had made them rejoice with great joy; the women and children also rejoiced. And the joy of Jerusalem was heard far away. (Neh 12:43)

After the completion of the wall around Jerusalem, the people prepared for a time of dedication. According to Mervin Breneman, it was "cause for celebration . . . music filled the air, and there was great joy."[73] Large processions filled the streets of Jerusalem as the people rejoiced before the Lord.

---

73. Breneman, *Ezra, Nehemiah, Esther*, 264.

What Does the Bible Say About Intergenerational Worship?

The processions found their way to the temple where a service of worship and sacrifice ensued.

Nehemiah formed two choirs who, with their instrumentalists, climbed the walls to sing and play. Choirs and other musicians made music before the Lord and praised him. Nehemiah records that the cacophony was so overwhelmingly loud that "the joy of Jerusalem was heard far away" (Neh 12:43). The people, according to Allen Ross, were "trying to recapture the spirit and the form of worship as it was legislated by Moses, developed by David, and reformed by Hezekiah and Josiah."[74] God's people were trying to rekindle the passionate worship that had existed in Jerusalem before the exile. Breneman also concurs—by striving to follow the prescription of worship Moses and David instituted, Nehemiah was reminding the people that they were part of an historical fabric of worship that transcended many generations.[75] Among the voices lifted in praise, Nehemiah records that the *women and children* also rejoiced. As the children participated in praise of God, they became part of that same fabric of worship—they found their place, among many generations, in God's ongoing plan.[76]

Concluding Thoughts

From the opening verses of Gen 1, God firmly established the pattern and the necessity of worship within community. God created humankind to exist in fellowship with him, and when Adam and Eve sinned, that fellowship was broken. However, God still provided a way, through worship, for man to reconnect, to recover a semblance of what was lost. God also made it clear that the burden for instructing future generations in the ways, character, and nature of God firmly rested on the shoulders of the family leaders. One generation was to commend God's works to the next as Ps 145 tells us. With that in mind, let us now turn our attention to the Psalms and see what we can glean regarding worshiping within the context of an intergenerational community.

---

74. Ross, *Recalling the Hope of Glory*, 353.
75. Breneman, *Ezra, Nehemiah, Esther*, 266.
76. Breneman, *Ezra, Nehemiah, Esther*, 266.

The Old Testament

QUESTIONS FOR THOUGHT AND DISCUSSION

1. God established the revelation/response pattern for worship at creation. How are we encouraging all generations present in our weekly worship gatherings to engage in this biblical pattern of worship?

2. In the Shema and other passages in Deuteronomy, God gave us a practical plan for discipling the next generation. How are the families in our church executing God's plan? How can we, as a church, come alongside our families and equip them to be the lead disciplers of their children?

3. We find in Joshua and Judges that the children of Israel were just one step away from slipping into idolatry. How are we standing in the gap for the emerging generations so that they do not suffer the same fate as Israel?

4. The Old Testament shows us that all generations benefit from being in worship together—young and old alike. How is my church encouraging this type of bidirectional discipling?

3

The Psalms

THE PSALMS HAVE ALWAYS been a treasure trove for worship. For millennia, the church has found the fabric, the substance, and the structure for worship within the pages of the Psalter. In the introduction to his three-volume commentary on the Psalms, author and scholar Allen Ross states that the Psalms have been the essence of the worship life for God's people for generations on end—with its "array of prayers, praises, hymns, meditations, and liturgies [that] cover all the aspects of living for God."[77] Ross continues that the Psalms should be informational in doctrine, inspirational to exhortation, and formational in the believer's spiritual life.[78] If this is true, then there is much information that can be gleaned from the Psalms relating to worship, but more importantly for our study, the Psalms offer both examples of intergenerational worship and commands to do worship within an intergenerational community. As we have already seen, Ps 145 states one generation should impart the knowledge and fear of God to other generations. What else do the Psalms teach us about worshiping intergenerationally?

REMEMBER AND TURN TO THE LORD

> Prosperity shall serve him; it shall be told of the Lord to the coming generation; they shall come and proclaim his righteousness to a people yet unborn, that he has done it. (Ps 22:30–31)

77. Ross, *Commentary on the Psalms*, 1:25.
78. Ross, *Commentary on the Psalms*, 1:25–26.

The opening words of Ps 22 are used by Christ on the cross—"My God, my God, why have you forsaken me?" (see Matt 27:46 and Mark 15:34). While this psalm has an obvious christological emphasis, it is the concluding expression of praise by the psalmist that is most relevant for our study of how the generations should interact in worship. Look closely at the final few verses. Here, the psalmist describes how he is eventually delivered from death and therefore praises God for his deliverance (Ps 22:21–31).

In his declaration of praise, the psalmist recounts God's goodness in delivering him from death at the hands of his enemies. Much like Ps 67, the psalmist proclaims that because of the retelling of the goodness and greatness of God, "all the ends of the earth shall remember and turn to the Lord" (22:27). It is in retelling the stories of God's righteousness (see Deut 6:4–9) by which others will learn of God. Then, in the final two verses of the psalm, he exhorts the current generation to "proclaim his righteousness to a people yet unborn" (22:31). Ross posits that God's people serve him by teaching their children about what God has done.[79] In essence, the psalmist is proclaiming that, as the nature of God's righteousness is proclaimed, mankind will be drawn to him. As one generation recounts the righteousness of God to succeeding generations, they will "turn to him in faith and become his witnesses to their generations."[80] In other words, one generation must remain faithful to transmit the nature and ways of God to succeeding generations.

Come, Children, and Listen

> Come, O children, listen to me; I will teach you the fear of the Lord. (Ps 34:11)

Psalm 34 is instructional for the worshiping congregation. Ross declares that "everyone should participate in telling the deeds of the Lord because telling them focuses attention on the greatness of the Lord, hence, he is magnified in the hearing of the people."[81] It is the focus on telling and teaching that is apropos to this study.

In verse 11, David offers the command to come and listen. The command to listen carries with it a connotation of learning and obeying. While

---

79. Ross, *Commentary on the Psalms*, 1:547.
80. Ross, *Commentary on the Psalms*, 1:547.
81. Ross, *Commentary on the Psalms*, 1:749.

the delineation of "children" (literally *sons*, בָּנִים)[82] in this passage may refer to the people at large as is found in Proverbs, it denotes those who are less mature in the faith.[83] In essence, David is declaring the importance of those more mature instructing those who are less mature in the nature, ways, and fear of God. While this may be accomplished within a singular generation, there is an undertone that is expressly cross-generational and intergenerational in nature.

PUT WORSHIP IN OUR BODIES

> Walk about Zion, go around her, number her towers, consider well her ramparts, go through her citadels, that you may tell the next generation that this is God. (Ps 48:12–13)

Psalm 48 is a declaration of praise to God who has done mighty acts. The psalm gives instruction for his people in liturgical ritual. Peter Craigie suggests that this instruction may have been initiated as part of the Feast of Tabernacles.[84] Craigie further contends that while Western Christianity has reduced worship to merely words, the experience of the children of Israel included physical action within their ritual. He states,

> The people not only addressed God in words, but also engaged in action, walking around that real, but symbolic, mountain and thus somehow making more immediate their awareness of the reality of a God who is ultimately beyond the grasp of the human senses.[85]

The physicality of the ritual is tied to the exhortation to tell the next generation about the presence and nearness of God. We understand from child development specialists, and especially those who focus on musical development in children (e.g., Kodály, Orff, and Dalcroze), that putting music "into the body" is imperative for successful learning.[86] In other words, we create movement, whether it be hand gestures (e.g., solfège) or full-blown choreographed movements, to teach music and thus help our children place it deep in their hearts to remember it. After completing a week of leading Vacation Bible School music, I can whole-heartedly testify

---

82. Craigie, *Psalms 1–50*, 280.
83. See Prov 4:1; 5:7; 7:24; 8:32.
84. Craigie, *Psalms 1–50*, 352.
85. Craigie, *Psalms 1–50*, 355.
86. Allcock and Bridges, *How To Lead*, 69.

that the physicality of adding movement to music cements both the melody and the text in our memories—and not just for children. I have been waking up in the middle of the night all week long singing the songs and going through the movements.

The reason movement and music are so bound together is that God created mankind to function this way. When God commands the children of Israel to walk around the city, he is using innate, God-created abilities to reinforce what he is teaching. Throughout the course of Scripture, God calls his people to physically participate in worship. Think back to our discussion of Passover. The participants were to eat the meal while fully clothed and with their outer cloaks and shoes on—symbolically and physically reenacting the original exodus from Egypt. When we put it into our bodies, we remember it much more easily. In other words, when we link the theoretical with the physical, we increase the likelihood of remembering something long term. In verse 13, the psalmist reiterates a common theme within the psalms: one generation is admonished to relate the good news of God's presence to succeeding generations.

Using a Lifetime of Worship Experience

> O God, from my youth you have taught me, and I still proclaim your wondrous deeds. So even to old age and gray hairs, O God, do not forsake me, until I proclaim your might to another generation, your power to all those to come. (Ps 71:17–18)

Psalm 71 has specific generational undertones throughout the text. While not necessarily overt, the ramifications of the generational ideas described in this passage are very relevant to the discussion of the necessity to connect the generations in the modern church. Marvin Tate proclaims that Ps 71 is one of very few that were penned by someone of mature age.[87] He further contends that "advanced age has at least one major advantage: a long memory of God's presence and of being taught to understand the ways of God."[88] The long memory of God's presence gives the psalmist a lifetime of experiencing God's nature, character, and actions in practice. Therefore, he can better instruct the coming generations of God's nature and ways.

The pattern described in this psalm is archetypal for the modern church. To effectively train less mature believers, it is necessary to integrate

---

87. Tate, *Psalms 51–100*, 217.
88. Tate, *Psalms 51–100*, 218.

those who have attained a higher level of spiritual maturity with them. Ross states that "while it is important to bring young people, young families, into the Church to build for the future, that future will be shaped to a large degree by mature believers."[89] The psalmist's plea for God to strengthen him so that he might be able to proclaim God's nature and ways to the rising generation should be the prayer of all mature believers in the church.

God's Work Deserves Retelling— Over and Over!

> We will not hide them from their children, but tell to the coming generation the glorious deeds of the LORD, and his might, and the wonders that he has done. He established a testimony in Jacob and appointed a law in Israel, which he commanded our fathers to teach to their children, that the next generation might know them, the children yet unborn, and arise and tell them to their children. (Ps 78:4–6)

Psalm 78 is a historical psalm in which the numerous mighty acts of God are placed in stark counterpoint with Israel's faithlessness. The purpose of this psalm is to instruct the coming generations of Israel in the ways and mercy of God. Tate says that the "recitals of the history of Israel in the psalm are not intended, of course, as mere exercises in historical epic. The history is the essential story, the root story, from which Israel understands her life in every generation."[90] Psalm 78 was used as a recitation tool to reinforce the oral history of Israel. Ross posits that "carrying on the oral tradition was the covenant duty of every generation."[91] Parents were to instruct their children using this tool so that they would understand the mighty acts of God.

While the mighty acts of God are prominent, a second aspect of the instruction found in this psalm is understanding the people's response to God. The psalmist recounts the glorious works of God in protecting, defending, and providing for the children of Israel, but he also details the rebellion of God's people. God's people repeatedly turned away from him. While it is important to tell of the mighty acts of God to future generations, it is also imperative to promote the understanding of the consequences of sin. Ross states that the "people of God in every age need to rehearse

---

89. Ross, *Commentary on the Psalms*, 2:532.
90. Tate, *Psalms 51–100*, 295.
91. Ross, *Commentary on the Psalms*, 2:660.

The Psalms

God's wonderful works on their behalf; but they also need to be reminded that these works were quickly forgotten."[92] It is necessary to teach both the praise and the warning that is found in Ps 78.

Even Amid Devastation, Praise God!

> But we your people, the sheep of your pasture, will give thanks to you forever; from generation to generation we will recount your praise. (Ps 79:13)

Psalm 79 is a lament describing the events surrounding the destruction of Solomon's Temple in 586 BCE. Paralleling Ps 74, which also describes the destruction of the temple, Ps 79 focuses on the resulting destruction in the city of Jerusalem. It follows the normal pattern for psalms of lament: lament, prayer, and a promise to praise.

We can get so wrapped up in the recounting of the destruction that we may miss the wonderful promise the psalmist includes. The psalm concludes with a vow to praise. The psalmist states that "we your people, the sheep of your pasture, will give thanks to you forever; from generation to generation we will recount your praise" (79:13). Even in the midst of devastation, exile, and loss of life, God's people are focused on recounting his praise across the generations. The importance of retelling the oral history of God's faithfulness is even more poignant when set against the harsh reality faced by God's people in that day. Amid the suffering, God's people were to tell of his mighty acts and deeds. How much more so should we, generations removed from God's miraculous works in the Old Testament, remind ourselves and our children that God is a worker of miraculous things? God can take a sinful man wallowing in the depths of his depravity and restore him through the shed blood of Christ. God is still in the miracle business and our children will only hear if we teach them.

An Emphatic Command

> One generation shall commend your works to another, and shall declare your mighty acts. (Ps 145:4)

A focal passage for this study, Ps 145 is the only one that bears the title of "Praise," and is the final psalm in the psalter attributed to David. It is also

---

92. Ross, *Commentary on the Psalms*, 2:656.

What Does the Bible Say About Intergenerational Worship?

one of the eight acrostic psalms and forms the opening of the grand doxology consisting of the final five psalms in the psalter.

In verse 4, the psalmist proclaims that one generation is to "commend your works" and "declare your mighty acts." This statement sums up the generational acts listed in the remaining psalms. It is the responsibility of existing, mature generations to commend and declare the mighty works, acts, nature, character, ways, and fear of God to emerging generations.[93] There are no equivocations. The psalmist commands us to teach emerging generations. The Psalm ends with a command to praise: "Let all flesh [some translations state "everything that has breath"] bless his holy name forever and ever" (Ps 145:21). This command is no less emphatic than the one in verse 4. As we teach the coming generations about the nature, ways, and character of God, they will have no recourse except to sing his praise forever and ever.

EVERY TRIBE, TONGUE, ... AND AGE!

> Kings of the earth and all peoples, princes and all rulers of the earth! Young men and maidens together, old men and children! Let them praise the name of the LORD, for his name alone is exalted; his majesty is above earth and heaven. (Ps 148:11–13)

An exuberant proclamation of praise, Ps 148 follows the pattern of creation as it begins with the heavenly hosts (v. 2) and traverses down through creation to man (vv. 11–12). Allen Ross states that "this movement suggests that the praise on earth, in Israel especially, should echo the worship in heaven. The call for praise therefore unites all creation, addressing both rational and irrational elements."[94] Young men and maidens, old men and children together are to praise the Lord together. There is no division or age segregation described in this passage—they are to praise the name of the LORD together. Matthew Henry suggests,

> Those of each sex, *young men and maidens*, who are accustomed to make merry together; let them turn their mirth into this channel; let it be sacred, that it may be pure. Those of each age. *Old men* must still bring forth this fruit in old age, and not think that

---

93. The word *declare* used here (נגד) is also the same used in Ps 22:31, which reads "they shall come and *proclaim* his righteousness to a people yet unborn, that he has done it" (emphasis added).

94. Ross, *Commentary on the Psalms*, 3:943.

either the gravity or the infirmity of their age will excuse them from it; *and children* too must begin betimes [or early] to praise God; even *out of the mouth of babes and sucklings* this good work is perfected.[95]

One can imagine that the ongoing praise in heaven is intergenerational as all generations of every nation, tribe, and tongue express praise and honor to God. Robert Pendergraft offers that "God's mercy and provision applies to people of all ages and both genders. It is right then for all men, women, and children to praise God."[96] From beginning to end, the texts of the Psalms are clear—regardless of age, mankind is to praise God, and it is the spiritual responsibility of older, more mature generations to impart the knowledge of God to succeeding generations.

---

95. Henry, *Job to Song of Solomon*, 643.
96. Pendergraft, "Credobaptist Defense," 74.

4

The New Testament

WHILE GOD ESTABLISHED THE PATTERN for worship in the Old Testament, the New Testament further refines God's design and helps us to understand the role of the church in light of Christ's coming. We will soon see that the role of the New Testament church, its purpose if you will, should be making disciples. Because of this purpose, we will spend our time focusing on the generational nature of making disciples as outlined within the pages of the New Testament. You may ask, "Why study making disciples? Why not just look at examples of worship?" The answer is simple. We will learn that worship and making disciples are inextricably linked together. While our main focus in worship is the exaltation of the Triune God of the universe, there is an element of spiritual formation that occurs in worship that just cannot be overlooked. Therefore, we will closely examine many passages that speak to the intergenerationality of disciple making and how it so seamlessly ties into the worship life of the church. Remember, while the words "intergenerational worship" do not ever appear in Scripture, we will discover the patterns of generational relationships as they relate to both worship and spiritual formation. These patterns are seen over and over and over again in context of the church, and are no more evident than in the life and ministry of Jesus Christ. As we examine his example, we will better understand the importance that Christ placed on relationships between the generations. Once we grasp those concepts, we will apply them to the discussion of contemporary church worship in later chapters.

The New Testament

INTERGENERATIONALITY IN THE LIFE AND MINISTRY OF JESUS

The Feeding of the Five Thousand

> And those who ate were about five thousand men, besides women and children. (Matt 14:21)

The only miracle recorded in each of the four gospels was Jesus feeding the five thousand. This miracle has an element of generationality that is often overlooked. The crowds who gathered around Jesus to hear his teaching were made up of many generations. Crowds of people from surrounding areas would make their way to wherever Christ might be teaching. In this particular instance, a very large crowd gathered on the mountainside. While there may be some confusion in speculating the number of different generations present, Matthew tells us they were there, and they were participating.[97] The loaves and fish that were to be the beginning of the miracle performed by Jesus were brought by a small boy (John 6:9). This miracle outlined in the Gospels evidences the way Christ ministered to the crowds. And in this event, as a child played a crucial role, assumptions can be made that other children were present in the multitudes around Jesus. Every place Jesus went he was followed by crowds made up of young people, children, and adults.

Let the Little Children Come

> Then the children were brought to him that he might lay his hands on them and pray. The disciples rebuked the people, but Jesus said, "Let the little children come to me and do not hinder them, for to such belongs the kingdom of heaven." (Matt 19:13–14)[98]

Matthew includes one of the most popular events in the life and ministry of Christ that is used when talking about including multiple generations in worship. In this instance, we see Christ's passionate response to the presence of children. Imagine the scene with me. Jesus has been preaching and teaching in Galilee. He and his disciples then traveled to Judea, and Scripture tells us that he was followed by large crowds (Matt 19:2). While

---

97. See Pendergraft, "Credobaptist Defense," 76–77.

98. The same incident is recorded in the other synoptic gospels. See Mark 10:13–16 and Luke 18:15–17.

What Does the Bible Say About Intergenerational Worship?

in Judea, the Pharisees tested Jesus with questions about divorce. As he was teaching, parents began to bring their children to Jesus for a blessing. I can just imagine what was happening: a very timid father places a small child within Jesus's reach—hoping that the Master would bless the child. As he did so, other parents who didn't want to miss out brought their children forward. In my mind's eye, I can see an onslaught of children being handed up to Jesus.

The disciples, who seem to be always concerned with unimportant details, begin to mutter among themselves. We can just hear them if we listen hard enough: "Who do these people think they are?" "Isn't the Master's time more valuably spent on those who can understand him?" "What's the deal with all these children?" Then their agitation turned into action and they began to try and stop what was happening. Not only did they try and stop it, they berated the parents for "getting in the way" of what they felt was really, truly important. When the disciples rebuked the people for disturbing the Master with children, Jesus was quick to respond, "Let the little children come to me" (Matt 19:14). But Jesus then escalated the situation. Not only did he embrace the children, but he also rescinded the disciple's rebuke and turned it back on them: "Do not hinder them, for to such belongs the kingdom of heaven" (Matt 19:14). Jesus's statement is in harmony with the thrust of the whole Scripture. As has been outlined previously, the scriptural role of a parent is to bring their children to an understanding of the nature, character, and ways of God. In other words, a parent's responsibility was to bring their children to Jesus, and Jesus reinforces this divine calling here. Matthew Henry states, "Those who glorify Christ by coming to him themselves, should further glorify him by bringing all they have, or have influence upon, to him likewise," and this most certainly includes children.[99] Whatever the circumstance, the essence of Christ's interchange with those present was to encourage the parents in their primary role of disciple maker.

When viewed in conjunction with Matt 18:1–6, Jesus is also rebuking the current cultural conventions relating to adults and children.[100] The

---

99. Henry, *Matthew to John*, 219.

100. "At that time the disciples came to Jesus, saying, 'Who is the greatest in the kingdom of heaven?' And calling to him a child, he put him in the midst of them and said, 'Truly, I say to you, unless you turn and become like children, you will never enter the kingdom of heaven. Whoever humbles himself like this child is the greatest in the kingdom of heaven. Whoever receives one such child in my name receives me, but whoever causes one of these little ones who believe in me to sin, it would be better for him to have

Greco-Roman tradition devalued children, and yet Christ's command is to become like a child.[101] Therefore, in these two passages, Jesus is purposefully breaking with tradition and focusing on the importance of the child in Christian thought. By breaking with traditional norms, Christ is modeling the true nature of intergenerational discipleship in the church. Christ is encouraging the parents to bring the children to him—to make disciples of them. But he is also stating that parents and others in the older generations must learn from children. Christ is saying that to enter his kingdom, one must have a childlike faith, not a childish faith. From this passage, we can glean the importance Christ has placed on intergenerational relationships in the disciple-making process.

A Call to Disciple Making

> Go therefore and make disciples of all nations, baptizing them in the name of the Father and of the Son and of the Holy Spirit, teaching them to observe all that I have commanded you. And behold, I am with you always, to the end of the age. (Matt 28:19–20)

Not necessarily a passage commonly used to discuss the church's worship practice, The Great Commission in Matt 28:19–29 does, however, inform Christian worship. The command to baptize in the name of the Father, Son, and Holy Spirit reveals the essence of God's nature and characteristics through his name. Malcolm Yarnell contends that the Old Testament name of God—YHWH—at this moment was "replaced with 'the Father, the Son, and the Holy Spirit.'"[102] Brandon Crowe, associate professor at Westminster Theological Seminary, concurs, extolling the significance of the "singular name [that] encompasses Father, Son, and Spirit," claiming the usage of the definite article before each person highlights the otherness of each person of the Trinity.[103] Yarnell further contends that "baptism in the name of the three is an act of worshipping the one in three."[104] Here, Jesus is highlighting the concept of worshiping in community by pointing out the community that is ever present in the Triune Godhead. His final *earthly* commands

---

a great millstone fastened around his neck and to be drowned in the depth of the sea'" (Matt 18:1–6).

101. Anthony and Anthony, *Theology for Family Ministries*, 22.
102. Yarnell, *God the Trinity*, 18.
103. Crowe, "Trinity and the Gospel of Matthew," 42.
104. Yarnell, *God the Trinity*, 22.

to the church revolve around worshiping together. Just as his ministry on earth depicted over and over, Christ is calling the church to *be together* in worship. However, in these commands he does not stop with thoughts of community.

Harkening back to the Deuteronomic texts encouraging discipleship, Jesus also commands his followers to teach the new converts to "observe everything I have commanded you" (Matt 28:20). In these words, we find the essence of the mission and the purpose for the church. We, the church, are called to make disciples. That purpose is lived out in so many different ways: through mentoring, through one-on-one discipleship, through Bible study, but most important for our study together, it occurs when we worship together. These final words that Jesus speaks to his disciples impart a great challenge for the church and truly encapsulate all of what Christ has taught throughout his earthly ministry. As we continue to read through the New Testament, we see that Christ's command is carried out by the apostles and the New Testament church.

The New Testament Church and Intergenerational Worship

The Household Will Follow the Head

> And after she was baptized, and her household as well, she urged us saying, "If you have judged me to be faithful to the Lord, come to my house and stay." And she prevailed upon us. (Acts 16:15)

> Then he brought them out and said, "Sirs, what must I do to be saved?" And they said, "Believe in the Lord Jesus, and you will be saved, you and your household." (Acts 16:30–31)

> Crispus, the ruler of the synagogue, believed in the Lord, together with his entire household. And many of the Corinthians hearing Paul believed and were baptized. (Acts 18:8)

The book of Acts records three instances where the head of various families—Lydia, the Philippian jailer, and Crispus—came to a saving knowledge of Christ. With them, the remainder of their households also followed Christ. For our study, these events show us the impact of the home and family on disciple making. Scott Brown states that "the home was designed by God to be a place of ministry. . . . For the first three centuries of church history, churches met primarily in homes."[105] There were no formal structures for the New Testament church. They met where they could avoid the prevalent persecution of Christians. As one member of a family came to know Christ, the other family members began to see the impact of walking with Jesus. The began to also turn to Christ.

You may ask, "What is the relevance to our study of worshiping in an intergenerational community?" We can only assume that these households were made up of multiple generations of families—grandparents, parents, children, all living together as was the cultural custom of the day. As a result, Allen and Ross state that "all generations met together, breaking bread, praying together, ministering to one another in the context of the home."[106] In each of these instances recorded in Acts, Luke describes that the whole household believed and was saved. While we cannot be assured of the ages of the children in the home, all generations must have been present. In essence, Luke is saying that the church is to be made up of multigenerational families—grandparents, parents, and children.

The Trinity Models Worship in Community

> The grace of the Lord Jesus Christ and the love of God and the fellowship of the Holy Spirit be with [μετά] you all. (2 Cor 13:14)

Brian Rosner, Australian author and educator, proclaims that "the famous benediction at the end of 2 Corinthians reveals the Trinitarian basis for Paul's vision of the Christian life."[107] The final words of Paul's second epistle to the church at Corinth reveals much in light of how the relationality of the Trinity should affect our worship. First, the benediction answers the question of *who* should worship. Many times, modern worshipers become so enamored with the pragmatic aspects of worship—*how* to worship—that they lose one of the more important foci. In my Survey of Christian Worship course the other day, we began a discussion about the misplaced focus of modern worship leaders. We talked about how most worship leaders tend to jump straight to the *what* of worship before they even begin to consider the *who* or even the *why* of what we do in corporate worship. Paul's inclusion of the preposition *with* (μετά) in his benediction forever relationally

---

105. Brown, *A Weed in the Church*, 104.
106. Allen and Ross, *Intergenerational Christian Formation*, 83.
107. Rosner, "Paul and the Trinity," 128.

links the Father, Son, and Holy Spirit with the worshipers. To display the current cultural relevance, the new parent company of Facebook is now called Meta—the Greek word (μετά) for "with."

The need to live and work in community is an inbred need for human existence. Malcolm Yarnell contends that humans respond in worship to God because he has initiated the relationship with them. He states, "The knowledge of *who* God is, the so-called immanent Trinity, comes to us through the experience of *how* God relates to us, the so-called economic Trinity."[108] In essence, Yarnell is saying that worshipers know God by how he relates to them. The immanent, or ontological Trinity is *ad intra*, or concerned with the internal relations within the Godhead. The economic Trinity is *ad extra*, or concerned with the external relationship of the Godhead to his creatures.[109]

The relational qualities of the Trinity, both *ad intra* and *ad extra*, have an incalculable impact on corporate worship. First, Deut 5:7–11 is clear that worship is to be given to God alone. Yarnell states that God "jealously requires the first and unique place in his people's hearts,"[110] but that worship is to be shared among the three, Father, Son, and Spirit. Therefore, worship of the one becomes worship of the one-in-three concurrently. Second, the relational aspect of the benediction has both a vertical and a horizontal component. Rosner states, "This fellowship, or participation, extends both to our relationship to God and to each other in the church. There is no autonomous life for the Christian, either horizontally or vertically without reference to the God known in Christ."[111] Third, salvation allows the believer to enter into "an eternal relation with Triune God."[112] The relational nature of the Trinity becomes the relational nature of the believer's worship. Yarnell summarizes the relationality of worshiping the Trinity by proclaiming, "To worship God correctly is to worship him as three-in-one with our whole mind, indeed with our whole being."[113] The totality of the believer's being is to enter into relationship and worship the totality of the Trinity.

---

108. Yarnell, *God the Trinity*, 35.
109. Yarnell, *God the Trinity*, 35.
110. Yarnell, *God the Trinity*, 45.
111. Rosner, "Paul and the Trinity," 128.
112. Yarnell, *God the Trinity*, 52.
113. Yarnell, *God the Trinity*, 55.

The New Testament

Strangers and Aliens in Our Midst

> So then you are no longer strangers and aliens, but you are fellow citizens with the saints and members of the household of God. (Eph 2:19)

While at first glance Eph 2:11–22 speaks of strangers and aliens in worship, there are some deeper ramifications as we consider this Scripture in light of intergenerational worship. There are very evident parallels that can be drawn between cultural differences and multiple generations worshiping together. In his doctoral project, Ray Crawford states that his church was battling to unify people across different cultures. However, in Crawford's church "the cultural barriers were caused not by separation of place or race, but by separation of time."[114] Cultural barriers can go beyond simple concepts of race or nationality. Each generation has a specific culture that is inclusive of customs, hierarchy, and even language. The more distantly removed a generation—for example, a member of the Builder Generation and a Millennial—the more their different backgrounds, life experiences, and cultural mores must be overcome to become fellow citizens. It only takes a brief conversation with a member of Generation Z to realize that, while we may speak the same base language, there is a distinct disconnect between my English as a Gen Xer and their chosen way to communicate. In this passage, Paul teaches that overriding cultural differences is both possible and necessary. Whatever issues seek to divide us, the church must learn to overcome and walk arm-in-arm as we seek to disciple the nations.

The Role and Call of the Young

> Children, obey your parents in the Lord, for this is right. "Honor your father and mother" (this is the first commandment with a promise), that it may go well with you and that you may live long in the land. Fathers, do not provoke your children to anger, but bring them up in the discipline and instruction of the Lord. (Eph 6:1–4)

> Wives, submit to your husbands, as is fitting in the Lord. Husbands, love your wives, and do not be harsh with them. Children, obey your parents in everything, for this pleases the Lord. Fathers,

---

114. Crawford, "For All Generations," 52.

> do not provoke your children lest they become discouraged. (Col 3:18–21)

Ephesians 5 through 6 is one of several passages where Paul outlines the roles of the New Testament household. He discusses the relationship between husband and wife at length, and then turns to the relationship between child and parent. The role of the parent is again outlined to be that of a disciple maker for their children—one who will "bring them up in the discipline and instruction of the Lord" (Eph 6:4). Joel Beeke posits that this passage parallels Deut 11:18–19 in that the words of God should be in father's hearts, and which they in turn must seek to teach to their children.[115]

While a cursory reading may simply give understanding to the earthly roles of parents and children, we can also find an eternal aspect to Paul's discourse. Andrew Lincoln states that Paul's description of the temporal family is "closely related to what he [Paul] has said earlier in the letter about the relationship of Christ and the Church and about the Church's calling in the world."[116] Robert Pendergraft further explains, "The household or family unit, was created to establish relationships that could be understood as types of the manner in which God through Christ relates to the church and individual believers."[117] The family, as the building block of earthly relationships, should help believers understand the complexity of their relationship to God the Father and also to other believers.

Paul further refines his assertions on the roles of the family in Col 3. Michael and Michelle Anthony suggest two theological principles from these two passages. First, the Christian home should be ordered in the way God designed.[118] The family provides a primary setting where spiritual discipleship can occur. The spiritual maturation of the next generation is more conducive when parents mentor children and children respond positively. Second, families should conform to God's design regardless of the current cultural circumstances.[119] In a culture that is rapidly moving away from Christian mores, the Christian family stands against the tide, and in doing so, reveals some of the nature and character of God to the unbelieving world. The Anthonys conclude, "If families fail, people have a much harder time understanding God and coming to him. . . . Every family bears the

---

115. Beeke, *Family Worship*, 11.
116. Lincoln, *Ephesians*, 352.
117. Pendergraft, "Credobaptist Defense," 61.
118. Anthony and Anthony, *Theology for Family Ministries*, 104.
119. Anthony and Anthony, *Theology for Family Ministries*, 104.

responsibility of looking like God."[120] The witness of the Christian family is an integral part of making disciples.

Even the Young Can Have a Spiritual Impact

> Let no on despise you for your youth, but set the believers an example in speech, in conduct, in love, in faith, in purity. (1 Tim 4:12)

In the final verses of 2 Tim 4, Paul exhorts Timothy, one of his students in the ministry, to stand firm and resolute in his ministry despite his young age. Paul encourages Timothy to live a life that is above reproach so that no one may be able to dismiss him out of hand. According to Paul, Timothy is to be an example to others—even in his youth. While Paul is addressing his comments directly to Timothy, his words can also be applied to the church. The church should look to the content and conviction of the heart rather than the chronological age or generational cohort. Older generations may be further matured through mentoring relationships with those who are younger. God used Timothy, despite his youth, to increase the faith of the church. We will see in the coming chapters that God uses both the old and the young in mentoring relationships. Many times, we only see mentorship happening in a top-down relationship—young people learning from older, wiser adults. While this can and is often true, adults can also be spiritually formed by the young.

A few years ago, a young girl connected to our church came to know Christ in a dynamic way. She had not been raised in the church and her family had no connection to the church or to Christ. But as a result of the Holy Spirit's moving after attending children's camp and Vacation Bible School one summer, this third-grade girl surrendered her life to Christ. She became one of the most avid and effective evangelists I have ever seen in over thirty years of ministry. Her entire family as well as many of her friends came to know Christ over the next several months. This nine-year-old modeled effective interpersonal evangelism in ways that encouraged and challenged even the most stalwart church members. Spiritual formation and mentorship is definitely a two-way street.

---

120. Anthony and Anthony, *Theology for Family Ministries*, 105.

What Does the Bible Say About Intergenerational Worship?

Families and Godly Role Models

> I am reminded of your sincere faith, a faith that dwelt first in your grandmother Lois and your mother Eunice and now I am sure, dwells in you as well. (2 Tim 3:5)

> But as for you, continue in what you have learned and have firmly believed, knowing from whom you learned it and how from childhood you have been acquainted with the sacred writings, which are able to make you wise for salvation through faith in Christ Jesus. (2 Tim 3:14–15)

The importance of familial relationships cannot be understated in the role of discipling the next generation—Timothy being a quintessential example. Timothy grew up in a household of faith. Paul records that both Timothy's mother and grandmother were women of faith. Author, generational strategist, and creator of Legacy Ministries Brian Haynes states that "God is the architect of the brilliant plan to capture the hearts of the generations. . . . God designed the family as the vehicle to pass on a heritage of faith, a godly legacy to the next generation."[121] Haynes believes that parents can fulfill their purpose by living out faithful lives in front of their children. Families, and especially parents, must model loving God for the next generation to fully understand.[122]

In verses 14 and 15, we find that Timothy learned the Scriptures from childhood. He was acquainted with the knowledge and ways of God from an early age because he was surrounded by those who lived out their faith in front of him. He saw the faith lived out by his mother and grandmother. His knowledge of Scripture and the demonstration of the faith in practice by his mother and grandmother formed the foundation on which Timothy came to understand his need for faith. The influence of godly role models in the nuclear family is so important to the spiritual growth. We have seen over and over throughout Scripture that God is using the family as the foundational building block by which emerging generations come to learn about him and follow him. Even more so, I believe that the concept of the family as spiritual role models also transfers to the church to some extent. Allow me to introduce it in this way: when the church either consciously or unconsciously divides their congregations by age, they are, in effect, removing much of the possibility for cross-generational spiritual formation. As

---

121. Haynes, *Legacy Path*, 4.
122. Haynes, *Shift*, 34.

we will discover in later chapters, while the family is the primary building block instructing emerging generations, the broader family of Christ found in the local church has an indescribably important impact in the discipling of future generations of believers.

A Biblical Summation of Intergenerational Spiritual Discipleship

> But as for you, teach what accords with sound doctrine. Older men are to be sober-minded, dignified, self-controlled, sound in faith, in love, and in steadfastness. Older women likewise are to be reverent in behavior, not slanderers or slaves to much wine. They are to teach what is good, and so train the young women to love their husbands and children. (Titus 2:1–4)

Titus 2 is a good summation of the biblical content relating to God's design for intergenerational relationships. In this passage, Paul briefly describes the characteristics of different generations—older men, older women, younger men, younger women—and discusses the relationship between each. Paul says the older generation is to be sober-minded, dignified, self-controlled, sound in faith, sound in love, and steadfast (Titus 2:2). He states the younger generation is to be self-controlled, dignified, a model of good works, and sound of speech (Titus 2:6–7). According to Paul, the result of proper generational relationships will be the training up of the future generations in right living (Titus 2:12–14).[123]

Scott Brown proposes that this passage also clearly communicates the intergenerational nature of the New Testament church. He states,

> Throughout the New Testament, social life in the early church was characterized by intergenerational relationships. The older teach the younger in intergenerational, personal relationships, rather than the young being gathered by themselves to be instructed in their peer groups. The richness of these relationships is pictured in Paul's relationship with younger men.[124]

---

123. Paul states the culmination of proper generational alignment to be "training us to renounce ungodliness and worldly passions, and to live self-controlled, upright, and godly lives in the present age, waiting for our blessed hope, the appearing of the glory of our great God and Savior Jesus Christ, who gave himself for us to redeem us from all lawlessness and to purify for himself a people for his own possession who are zealous for good works" (Titus 2:12–14).

124. Brown, *A Weed in the Church*, 119.

What Does the Bible Say About Intergenerational Worship?

Brown notes that there is no supposition of "systematic, age-segregated, peer-group-oriented training"[125] functioning within the context of the New Testament church as described in Titus. Conversely, Titus 2 indicates that discipleship can truly blossom when the generations have substantial interaction with each other. Allow me to explain this concept with the following story from the life of Christ.

This past Sunday was the first Sunday following Christmas. Our pastor focused our church's attention in a little different way this year. Instead of the typical looking ahead to the new year and to the goals that we should and would set, he focused on that part of Christ's earthly life that is often overlooked—those years between his birth and ministry—his childhood. He taught from Luke 2:40–52 and what happened when twelve-year-old Jesus remained at the temple while his family began to make their way home following the Passover celebration. There are some great intergenerational concepts to be found in this short passage and they have direct ties to the passage in Titus 2 and help to give a summary of what I believe the entirety of Scripture is trying to teach about intergenerational relationships and their importance to worship.

The gist of the story in Luke 2:40–52 is that a large group from Nazareth had traveled to Jerusalem to celebrate the Passover as they did every year (Luke 2:41). First of all, notice that it was a regular occurrence. The family would pack up and make the long journey to Jerusalem to celebrate the Passover every year. It wasn't something that was haphazard. No, they would intentionally put forth the effort to worship in the way God had prescribed. This single statement begins to show us the importance of worship even in the early life of Jesus.

The story then continues by recounting that on the way back to Nazareth, Mary and Joseph didn't realize that Jesus wasn't with them because they were traveling with a large group of family and friends. They thought that he might be with aunts, uncles, cousins, or neighbors. In other words, they didn't participate in worship just as a family but as a community of worshipers. There were so many people traveling that Jesus's parents assumed he was in the convoy somewhere. Our pastor summarized the story by concluding that the church today should be like that traveling group. It should be a big part of the community of faith, not just within the walls of the church, but in the everyday lives of believers. This tight-knit group of travelers walked together, talked together, ate together, and worshiped

---

125. Brown, *A Weed in the Church*, 121.

together. They were using the power of intergenerational relationships to make an impact on the spiritual development of all their children. In my opinion, that is a great picture of what the church should be today.

Concluding Thoughts

The teaching of Scripture is clear: God created man to be relational—with each other and with God. Over and over, throughout Scripture, the generations are together for worship and for instruction. However, current culture favors systems of age segregation—ministry silos in which we can relegate the instruction of future generations to paid professionals. The concept of a society completely organized around small peer groups is a new cultural construct that, as we have seen, is at odds with biblical teaching. There are times when small peer groups can be effective, and those instances will be discussed in later chapters. However, when the church gathers for worship, there is benefit, designed by God and supported by Scripture, to the whole church gathering together. Younger generations are affected by the wisdom and maturity of the older generation, while those more mature may be affected by the passion and vigor of youth. Modern worship planners and leaders should intentionally account for intergenerational connections in worship. Incorporating intentional mutuality in the planning and execution of worship will help to bring clarity to intergenerational connections in worship. As outlined in the biblical texts, the generations need each other in worship.

The Trinity also affords a distinctive model for relationships within the church and the family. Believers come to know God's three-in-one nature expressed in his name and through the relational interaction of Father, Son, and Spirit. God's design for the family can then come to fruition—the dominion mandate to multiply and bear spiritual fruit is fulfilled and making disciples becomes paramount in day-to-day family life. The multigen worship concept emerging within worship leadership circles evidences the current church culture's perceived need to return to a more biblical model. In the coming chapters, we will discover ways to begin to heal the divisions and put the generations back together for worship.

What Does the Bible Say About Intergenerational Worship?

QUESTIONS FOR THOUGHT AND DISCUSSION

1. Is my church following the biblical pattern for worship within the context of an intergenerational community?

2. As a church leader, am I doing everything I can do to encourage, equip, and prepare adults to connect to younger generations effectively and intentionally?

3. What do the Scriptures we've studied reveal that I must do in my current ministry role? How can I act upon God's plan for intergenerational worship in the church in which he has placed me?

4. What is a first, small step I can take as a ministry leader to move my congregation to be more aware of its biblical mandate to make disciples of every generation?

PART TWO

Why Does Worshiping Intergenerationally Really Matter?

> Our segregated performance-oriented worship leads to a loss of focus on the worship of God as the gathering of the whole body of believers. Furthermore, it tears at the fabric of families. In contrast, corporate and participatory worship, where families are in the same community worshiping together, has the unintended side benefit of strengthening the shared faith of families.
>
> DIANA GARLAND, *FAMILY MINISTRY*

5

What Is Intergenerational Worship?

THE MEGACHURCH IS BOOMING these days. In our metropolitan area, churches that seek to target specific age groups—namely young families with children—seem to be growing at an astonishing rate. Parents who want their children to be in the *best*, most attractive children's ministry tend to church hop until they find somewhere with all the razzle and dazzle to keep their kids entertained and wanting to come back. If these types of ministries are thriving, why do we even want to take another look way back to how they were doing church before the current generation? First and foremost, because it is the way God intended for us to be the church. Second, as we strengthen family ties, we build up not only our community of faith but our whole community. Third, if we really look—if we remove all the glitz and glamour—are these churches really thriving? Are they fulfilling the primary mission of the church in making disciples, or are they simply entertaining an audience?

As our congregations are beginning to seek to become more intergenerational, a logical first step in the process would be to intentionally rethink the way we are "doing" worship. Are we being intentional as we seek to incorporate all the generations? In many churches—even those who are age-segregated in most ministries—the corporate worship service may be the single remaining weekly event when all the generations are together in the same place at the same time. As we discovered in part one, Scripture tells us that God designed and created us to worship in community, and that community of faith helps to shape and form us into the image of Christ. As leaders, we should leverage these times of worship to forge

Why Does Worshiping Intergenerationally Really Matter?

intergenerational connections that can encourage spiritual formation. But before our churches can realize the benefits of intentionally focusing on generational connectedness, we must first understand what true intergenerational worship really looks like.

Who Should Be Present in Worship?

When I begin to think about intergenerational involvement, my mind automatically turns to all those holidays when I was growing up. You remember those days, hopefully, when family from all over the place would come together. Since my immediate family was a "ministry" family, it seemed as if we would always have to travel to wherever we were celebrating the holidays that year. Some of the fondest memories of my childhood were those spent with cousins, aunts, uncles, grandparents, and others enjoying one another's company.

However, when it came time to eat, that was a different story. I remember looking at the beautiful table set with all the fine china and crystal. My grandmother had the most beautiful red crystal stemware (that have now passed down to me). I would love looking at the beautiful place settings and imagining that I was eating with royalty. When it was time to sit down, however, we kids were always relegated to the dreaded "kid's table." It was always a bare little table with none of the finery that you saw on the adult table. In those moments, I longed for the time that I would graduate to the adult table. It eventually happened, and I loved every minute of it. But for all those years at the kid's table, while I had a good time with the cousins, I felt disconnected from the *real* celebration.

In much the same way, when we segregate our children and young people from corporate worship, we are disconnecting them from the body as a whole. They see their peers, and they have a great time playing games, singing songs, and having a little Bible study, but they miss out on the true meat of the feast! They are eating on the proverbial paper plates, while the adults sample the real fare. I believe that God has called us to be different!

While we've learned that there is no biblical description of intergenerational worship, the practice of worship in Scripture consistently shows all generations participating together.[126] As Nehemiah finished reconstructing the wall around Jerusalem, he gathered all the people, old and young, to both celebrate and hear the Law of God read (Neh 8:1–3; 12:43). In

---

126. Aniol, *Let the Little Children Come*, 20.

What Is Intergenerational Worship?

Deuteronomy, God specifically delineates who is to be present in the corporate worship of Israel: "Assemble the people, men, women, and little ones, and the sojourner within your towns, so that they may hear and learn to fear the Lord your God" (Deut 31:12).[127] In a time of crisis (Joel 2), God called on all people—elders, children, and even nursing infants—to gather in repentance, fasting, and solemn assembly. In Matt 19, Jesus used the example of children in the worshiping community. In Acts 20, the story of Eutychus also indicates that young people were welcomed to participate in New Testament worship, and we'll have more to say about Eutychus in chapter 7. Over and over in Scripture, God planned for the generations to worship together. With that understanding firmly in hand, let's seek to define true intergenerational worship.

Defining Worship

Understanding the nature of intergenerational worship necessitates a firm grasp on the meaning and practice of worship in its entirety. Many Christian scholars have sought to define worship. James W. White proclaims that worship is "a multifaceted, multimedia, multimeaningful human activity. . . . The purpose of our gathering as Christians, is meeting to the praise of God by the people of God. But while this meeting and praise is occurring, people are formed by their worship."[128] White is clear: worship is to praise God. Moreover, both White and Holly Allen contend that worship is a formational activity for the people of God.[129] As God's people worship, the Holy Spirit transforms them more and more into the likeness of Christ. Another scholar, Bruce Leafblad, former professor of church music at Southwestern Baptist Theological Seminary, demanded all his students to memorize a definition of worship so that it would permeate their worship planning and leadership. I can still quote verbatim Leafblad's definition of worship some thirty-five years later. Leafblad states, "Worship is communion with God in which believers, by grace, center their mind's attention and their heart's affection on the Lord, humbly glorifying God in response to his greatness and his Word."[130] For Leafblad, a key aspect of worship was the communion that occurred within the dialogical nature of worship—God reveals

---

127. See also Deut 12:7–12; 16:11,14; 29:10–12.
128. White, *Intergenerational Religious Education*, 47.
129. Allen, "What Is Intergenerational Worship?"
130. Leafblad, "Philosophy of Church Music."

himself and man responds. With much the same thrust, Robert Pendergraft succinctly defines worship as "our response to God's revelation."[131]

From the outset, God created worship to be dialogical—a pattern of revelation and response. At creation, God made man in his image and man walked and talked with God (Gen 1:27; 3:8). The Creator could have waited for man to seek him out, but he did not. God revealed himself to Adam and Eve, and they communed together. God instituted the responsorial prototype for worship and man has sought to follow his plan ever since. As the children of Israel gathered and worshiped around Mt. Sinai, God again set a dialogical paradigm as the practice for Old Testament worship. Exodus 24 outlines six elements of worship that follow the dialogical narrative:

1. God reveals himself and calls the people to worship.
2. The people acknowledge God's call and make confession.
3. God offers atonement.
4. God proclaims his word.
5. The people respond in commitment.
6. God hosts a celebratory feast.
7. God's people respond to the action of God.

Worship cannot be initiated by man—only God can draw his people to worship. The prophet Isaiah continues to reiterate God's relational and dialogical plan for worship in Isa 6:1–8.[132] As we learned in part one, God also created worship to be done in the context of an intergenerational community. As God reveals himself, God's people—all God's people—respond to him.

What Is Intergenerational Worship?

Quite simply stated, intergenerational worship evokes scenes of children, students, and adults all worshiping, learning, and growing together. Diana Garland defines intergenerational worship as using representatives of all age groups to plan and lead worship times that stretch everyone yet

---

131. Pendergraft, "It's Not Just About the Children."

132. Isa 6:1–8: revelation, adoration, confession, expiation, proclamation, dedication, and commission.

What Is Intergenerational Worship?

yield times of feeling like each congregant truly belongs.[133] In Garland's view, intergenerational worship can occur when the whole congregation is involved in the pattern of revelation and response. There should be an element of intentionality when planning for the involvement of all the generations in worship. For example, children can read God's word, opening the eyes of the congregation to God's revelation of himself. Students can offer musical leadership. Adults and children can respond with hymns of joy or songs of lament and in times of confession. In chapter 7, we will closely examine the idea of intentional mutuality as a process to achieve what Garland describes.

A second important characteristic of intergenerational worship is one we also find in Garlands definition described above: a deep sense of feeling like you are at home. Think about a time when you have been away from home for an extended period. It may have been while you were attending college, tending to a sick relative, or just on a long vacation. A few weeks ago, my wife and I returned from an incredible vacation. We had been planning and looking forward to our trip for a long time. When we left home, there was a feeling of excitement and looming adventure. As our vacation was winding down, we began to long for home. I can tell you that a deep sense of comfort struck us as soon as we opened our door and walked into our home. We were so grateful for the chance to get away, but as the saying goes, there's no place like home.

That same feeling of belonging can occur as every generation is not only welcomed but invited to actively participate in every element of our worship services. There are many ways to accomplish this goal. For instance, we can use a child to welcome all worship participants, thereby encouraging the other children present to feel at home. A student reading Scripture or leading a biblical responsive reading helps students feel a part of the service. Including senior adults as well as young adults on the musical leadership teams helps their respective age groups feel represented and essential.

A sense of belonging can also be encouraged when a feeling of equality is shared among everyone in the congregation. Howard Vanderwell defines intergenerational worship as "worship in which people of every age are understood to be equally important."[134] We must be careful not to pander to specific age groups within the congregation. When we strictly

---

133. Garland, *Family Ministry*, 468.
134. Vanderwell, *Church of All Ages*, 11.

Why Does Worshiping Intergenerationally Really Matter?

target a generation, such as singing a "youth chorus," utilizing an ineffective children's sermon, or even throwing in a token "old hymn" to appease the senior adults, worship leaders may unconsciously communicate that the rest of the worship time was designed for someone else.

To promote a sense of equality and belongingness, every worship service element should be carefully crafted to engage members of all generations. Expounding on the sense of equality and belonging, Holly Allen contends that intergenerational worship is "where we value all ages, listening to, engaging with, bringing all into an encounter with God."[135] In other words, not only should church leadership value all ages, but worship planners should seek to engage them, bringing them into active participation in worship. For example, worship leaders should try to incorporate music that speaks the "heart language" of all those in the congregation. In part one we discovered that in Scripture, every generation was actively involved in the worship process. At Passover, the children had specific responsibilities to ask questions (Exod 12:26). In Joel 2, the children participated in fasting alongside their parents. In the New Testament, Christ used children as an example of true worshipers (Matt 19:14). When we value and involve members of every age group, we increase their sense of being at home.

The third defining characteristic of true intergenerationality is wrapped up in the other two. We, as worship planners and leaders, must encourage the active participation and engagement of all generations.[136] As we have already discussed, there is a big difference between multigenerational churches and intergenerational churches. Many, if not most, congregations today are multigenerational—they consist of members of many different generations. However, multigenerational churches do not necessarily encourage the active interplay of all generations present. To be truly intergenerational, there should be reciprocity, or a mutual exchange, between the multiple generations.[137] That exchange should go beyond the mere superficial—it's more than a greeting in the hallway or a nod across the room. The interaction must become an inclusion of all ages in the elements of worship every week.

---

135. Allen, "What Is Intergenerational Worship?"

136. Here Harkness states that the mutual contributions from the participation of all age groups enhance the spiritual formation of the body. Harkness, "Intergenerational Corporate Worship," 15.

137. Allen and Ross, *Intergenerational Christian Formation*, 17.

What Is Intergenerational Worship?

Taking these ideas into consideration, I believe we can now formulate a definition of intergenerational worship. In my opinion, intergenerational worship is corporate worship in which leaders seek to create opportunities that encourage spiritual formation and foster a sense of belonging as all generations engage in the pattern of revelation and response established and initiated by God. That may be a mouthful, but it encompasses the important identity of intergenerational worship. If we want to be truly intergenerational, we will need to involve people of all ages in planning, leading, and participating in worship *together*. It fulfills the mission of Prov 27:17[138] and creates opportunities for all generations to not only feel like they are an important part of the body but that they are part of something much more important—God's revelation of himself and his invitation for his children to respond to him in worship. In the next two chapters, we will unpack this new definition of intergenerational worship so that we can see how to encourage connections between the generations.

---

138. "Iron sharpens iron, and one man sharpens another." Here, the author expresses the results of connection. When we work, learn, and worship together, each of us is formed, or sharpened, by the other.

6

What's Really at Stake?

It seems as if many of our faith communities are moving toward a more intergenerational approach to ministry. We are beginning to see family-based ministry gain a foothold and become more commonplace. As more congregations seek to become intentionally intergenerational, I truly believe that we must first examine how we are worshiping. In many churches—even those who are overtly age-segregated in the majority of what they do—the corporate worship service may be the single remaining weekly event when all the generations come together. As we discovered in part one, Scripture reveals that God designed worship to be both intergenerational and formational for his people. Leaders should leverage these times of worship to deepen intergenerational connections that can encourage spiritual formation. But before they can realize the benefits of intentionally focusing on generational connections, leaders must first understand the biblical nature of intergenerational worship. To describe the necessity for intergenerational worship, I have examined the biblical and historical nature of worship in part one, and why it is so important to worship intergenerationally. In the following chapters, I will seek to describe what being intentionally intergenerational really looks like. Finally, we will examine a possible plan to begin to revive God's plan for intergenerational worship in our churches.

What's Really at Stake?

WHY THE DIVIDE?

Why does the contemporary church seek to divide along generational lines? There are many explicit and implicit reasons. First, age segregation can be used as a method of church growth. Gordon Smith states that separating church members by age "is an effective way to bring people in the door."[139] Timothy Paul Jones agrees, citing his early ministry where age-segregated ministry focused on increasing attendance numbers.[140] Many churches focus on the attraction quality of age-oriented ministry to bring in new people. These churches might build elaborate children's and student facilities in hopes of reaching the rest of the family. It is not uncommon to see churches whose children's ministry areas rival Disney. They will bring in design experts that will create a "magical" world where the kids will never want to leave. The same ideas are prevalent in student ministry. Some churches will build teen hangouts that include video game stations, full-service snack bars, and comfy seating. Are these developments a negative? Not necessarily, but allow me to paint a picture for you.

As Diana Garland has pointed out, age-oriented worship can negatively impact both the family and the church.[141] Think about this for a moment. You have a group of children who have graduated from an incredible preschool ministry. They are finally big enough to go to the kid's area. They may experience incredible Bible study and discipleship. They may also participate in a fast-paced, excitement-filled worship time that is geared specifically for them. The leaders automatically adjust their worship plan to accommodate for the typical short attention span of today's child. They play games, sing high-energy songs with scripted choreography, and they have time for a devotional thought and application. That sounds great, but let's continue with the scenario.

The children reach the age where they finally can move into the student ministry. Again, they have discipleship opportunities that are created specifically for them. They are encouraged and enriched by caring adult volunteers. Then the students move into a time of worship crafted for their tastes and needs. The planners concentrate on the developmental idiosyncrasies of the teenage years. They limit the focus time needed to accommodate for shorter attention spans. They include elements that will break

---

139. Smith, "Generation to Generation," 183.
140. Jones, *Perspectives on Family Ministry*, 7.
141. Garland, *Family Ministry*, 451.

Why Does Worshiping Intergenerationally Really Matter?

up time into smaller, more digestible pieces by using group games, object lessons, video, and other activities. The worship leaders only use the music that is currently in the top twenty-five of the CCLI charts. They incorporate significant lighting and special effects, and the music is led by a well-rehearsed, semi-professional worship team. There is an emotionally charged atmosphere, and the students overwhelmingly respond. Again, why should we complain? The students are hopefully delving deep into discipleship and are worshiping with abandon, but let's continue with the story.

The eighteen-year-old young adults have just graduated and spent their last summer in the student ministry. Now they have aged out and their only option for discipleship and worship in their church is "adult" Bible study and "adult" worship. Think about it. The church has been catering to these young adults since birth. They have adjusted everything they do to conform to the particular needs of the various stages of development. Suddenly, these young adults are thrust into a world that is not really designed for them. They have never been through a full worship service designed for adults. There are no games or other activities to hold their interest. There are no volunteers catering to their every need so that they can participate. They are alone, unprepared, and undiscipled. And they begin to slip away. We will discuss Ben Trueblood's research in chapter 9 but let me give you a preview. Ben has found that 66 percent of eighteen to twenty-two-year-olds who have not developed deep intergenerational connections will stop attending church.[142] To me, that figure is staggering, and it tells me that we are not doing a good job in connecting our children and students to the church as a whole.

As described in the stories above, age-segregated worship proponents seek to reach children and students more effectively by focusing ministry on their particular developmental age and stage. With social science advancements categorizing stages of development, many church leaders seek to create both discipleship and worship opportunities that cater to the different developmental/life stages.[143] Holly Allen and Christine Ross contend that developmental concerns prompted ministry leaders to "create

---

142. Trueblood, *Within Reach*, 12.

143. Church leaders have adapted research by various social scientists (e.g., Piaget, Kohlberg, Erikson, and others) to create appropriate activities, including discipleship and worship, for children and students coinciding with levels of cognitive and emotional development. See Allen and Ross, *Intergenerational Christian Formation*, 130–32; Smith and Denton, *Soul Searching*; May et al., *Children Matter*, 79–80; and Pendergraft, "Credobaptist Defense," 128–64.

more developmentally appropriate worship opportunities for children in order to bless them spiritually."[144] While age-segregated worship may bring short-term benefits such as increased attendance and excitement, dividing along developmental stages raises a serious theological question. If the church is to follow practices outlined in the Scripture, worship should be intergenerational. The issue is not psychological or developmental, but theological.[145] Allen suggests that in the church's current developmentally appropriate focus with children and young people, it has disregarded intergenerational worship's theological impact. Steve Burger, director of children and family ministry for Evangelical Covenant Church in Chicago, further suggests that the theological rationale for dividing along developmental lines may come from placing "emphasis on *learning about* faith over and above the importance of *participating in* faith."[146] The act of worship participation and developing a relationship *with* God far outweighs the knowledge *of* God. As we will learn, when we worship as God intended, we will experience great spiritual growth. God uses every generation to teach the others by modeling and mentoring, and by simply being together—sharing the same space and breathing the same air.

The experts truly speak with one voice: intergenerational worship deepens spiritual formation in all participants.[147] As Scripture has shown, God designed worship to be relational. The same concept can also be translated to discipleship. Scripture indicates that discipleship can best occur when generations mentor one another (Prov 27:17; 1 Tim 1:2; 2 Tim 1:2; Titus 2:1–8). An inherent theological problem of age-segregated worship and discipleship, according to Allen and Burger, happens when the absence of intergenerational relationships hampers spiritual formation.[148] Howard Vanderwell also tells us that church leaders must form a "culture of deep

---

144. Allen and Ross, *Intergenerational Christian Formation*, 195.

145. Allen states, "We asked too many psychological and developmental questions in the past. We need to ask the theological questions now." Allen, "Bringing Intergenerational Worship."

146. Burger, "It Takes a Congregation"; emphasis added.

147. Csinos and Beckwith state that worship that is intergenerational nurtures "the spiritual lives of children—and of people of all ages." Csinos and Beckwith, "Better Together," 37. Glassford states, "Worship that is genuinely intergenerational is best attempted in the context of efforts to create an entire ethos or culture of intergenerational relationships. Such an ethos will . . . encourage corporate spiritual formation." Glassford, "Fostering an Intergenerational Culture," 86.

148. Allen, "Bringing Intergenerational Worship"; Burger, "It Takes a Congregation."

Why Does Worshiping Intergenerationally Really Matter?

relationships in which we seek the good of others and respect one another regardless of age, sex, or any developmental considerations."[149] Why, you may ask? Because spiritual formation really matters. We, as the church, are called to make disciples of all people (Matt 28:19–20). Part of the disciple-making process is encouraging spiritual growth/formation. Church leaders should move past the issues of developmental concerns and understand that biblical worship that promotes spiritual formation involves every generation—together. One of the best ways to foster spiritual growth and formation is to equip the families in our churches to fulfill their task of making disciples both in the home and in the pew at church.

ENCOURAGING THE FAMILY AS DISCIPLE MAKERS

Diana Garland expresses another possible reason for age-segregated worship: distractions caused by unruly children. Garland explains that the easy solution some churches employ is to move younger or unruly children to a separate space where they won't be a distraction.[150] In doing so, moving children into a separate space for worship may become a matter of convenience for parents seeking escape from parental responsibility. Many churches allow parents to send their children and students to age-appropriate worship services so that the parent can focus his/her attention on adult matters and their individual spiritual growth. As they do so, parents can attend worship without dealing with unruly, unprepared, undisciplined, and undiscipled children. Through age-segregated worship, parents can forego what they might see as a difficult or time-consuming task: teaching their children how to worship. By using age-segregated worship, parents can allow trained professionals to assume the primary discipleship role while they move into supportive roles.[151] But Scripture tells us that this is not what God intended. As we have already discovered in part one, passage after passage commands parents to teach their children what it means to worship God.

These ideas beg us to answer another question: are all age-segregated ministries suspect? The answer is a resounding no. Utilizing *some* age-oriented activities in conjunction with focused intergenerational interaction times may help to bolster parents' efforts in discipleship.[152] Using existing

149. Vanderwell, *Church of All Ages*, 72.
150. Garland, *Family Ministry*, 451.
151. Anthony and Anthony, *Theology for Family Ministries*, 182.
152. See Strother, "Family-Equipping Ministry," 144. See also Jones, *Perspectives on*

age-oriented discipleship structures, like Sunday school, can offer times for training and discipling parents and giving support for the parent's discipleship efforts with their children. Therefore, John Roberto urges churches to find a balance between segregation and integration.[153] In most churches, the place that balance can be most easily achieved is in the weekly worship gathering.

There is still a problem, however. The weekly worship gathering in most churches is simply an extension of the age-segregation in other ministries. Students sit with and interact with only students. Senior adults congregate at the back of the worship center together. Families with elementary-age children may sit together, but they are not necessarily being intentional in instructing the children on their role in worship. And to make the problem worse, there are very few scholarly voices discussing the issues and offering suggestions to improve the situation.

Currently, the scope of literature dealing with intergenerational worship practices is very limited. While several studies focus specifically on how we can better involve children in worship, few studies discuss worship from the perspective of engaging believers of all ages. God calls all people to worship. As evidenced in Scripture and as discussed in the following chapter, when families gather together for worship, spiritual formation can more easily happen in the lives of children, teenagers, college students, young adults, median adults, and senior adults. As the body unites in worship, each generational segment brings different perspectives that can encourage and strengthen others. Richard Jackson, pastor emeritus of North Phoenix Baptist Church, once stated that when the church worships together, each participant brings unique characteristics and abilities gifted through the Holy Spirit to the meeting.[154] The Holy Spirit within each worshiper brings about formation and transformation in the lives of others, transforming them into the image of Christ. The principle of Prov 27:17 takes root as one believer disciples another.[155] The spiritual formation described by Pastor Jackson can occur when the church actively, intentionally, faithfully, and intergenerationally worships together. Allen and Ross concur and state,

---

Family Ministry, 40–41; Roberto, "Our Future Is Intergenerational," 110; Allen and Ross, *Intergenerational Christian Formation*, 47.

153. Roberto, "Our Future Is Intergenerational," 110.

154. Richard Jackson, interim pastor of Lakeside Baptist Church, Granbury, TX, in conversation with the author, 2008.

155. "Iron sharpens iron, and one man sharpens another" (Prov 27:17).

Why Does Worshiping Intergenerationally Really Matter?

"For intergenerational Christian formation to happen, the generations must *be* together; they must *know each other*, and they must experience life in the body of Christ *together*."[156] As the body worships and lives life together, it matures.

Children also need to *see* their parents and grandparents worship. They need to see older students who serve as role models worship. In his examination of children in Baptist worship, Adam Harwood, professor at New Orleans Baptist Theological Seminary, suggests that children learn as much from observation as they do from education.[157] Harwood states: "Children, like adults, can learn to follow Christ by watching other people follow Jesus. They can learn to pray, for instance, by listening to others pray. They can learn how to do justly and love mercy by watching someone lead a godly life."[158]

Likewise, adults need to see children worship. Something happens when a young person comes to salvation. There is an excitement, an overwhelming joy in worship that we adults need to see. When we do, we are encouraged to cry out to God for a restoration of the joy of our own salvation. Let me illustrate it this way. As I described in chapter 4, we had an older elementary child come to know Christ. As a result, she became the most prolific evangelist I had ever seen in over thirty years of ministry. She introduced family members—parents, aunts, uncles, cousins—to Jesus. She brought carloads of friends with her to almost every event the church sponsored. That small girl both encouraged and challenged the rest of us in our willingness to lay aside our fears and share the gospel with those around us. She helped us to grow . . . to mature in our faith. That formation would not have been possible if she had been relegated to children's church. The mothers and fathers, the grandparents, and even the students in attendance in our services were able to grow because we were active participants in her story. Enthusiasm and spiritual fervor can rub off on others just as much as wisdom does. Mentoring is not just a top-down affair. When we realize that we can be taught and encouraged by even the smallest of children, we will see a deepening of our own spiritual growth.

Our church has entered a special time of focusing on the generations in our worship services. In chapter 10, I will tell you more about what we started in our church a few summers ago. We were being intentional about

---

156. Allen and Ross, *Intergenerational Christian Formation*, 270.
157. Harwood and Lawson, *Infants and Children*, 181.
158. Harwood and Lawson, *Infants and Children*, 181.

putting the generations together for worship, and we are still reaping the rewards. Even now, several years later, we still have children joining us on our worship leadership teams because we showed them that they have a place—a role that only they can fulfill. As they do, the whole body of believers is encouraged. The adult members of our leadership teams are bolstered by the children's fervor, excitement, and spontaneity. The children are growing deeper by learning *how* to worship by those who have been worshiping for half a century or more. Therefore, I believe that we can say with some certainty that a key to spiritual formation can be found in the physical act of worshiping together—intergenerationally. But how can we make that happen? What does worshiping intergenerationally look like?

7

What Does Being Intentional Look Like?

GOD CREATED BOTH THE FAMILY and the church to encourage spiritual formation in the life of every believer—young and old.[159] As part one demonstrated, God intended spiritual formation to happen intergenerationally. Psalm 79:13 proclaims, "From generation to generation we will recount your praise." And Ps 145:4 commands, "One generation shall commend your works to another, and shall declare your mighty acts." Yet how can one generation influence another if there is no interaction or connection between them? To fully realize the impact of generational connectedness as demonstrated in Scripture, the church must move from being simply multigenerational to intentionally equipping, interconnecting, and engaging all generations, and it begins with the family.

As church members and families within the church mature physically, socially, and mentally, God intends for them to also grow spiritually (Gen 1:28). Scripture indicates that God created the family to be the core unit for discipleship. In Deut 4, 6, and 11, God instructs families to constantly teach their children about the nature and ways of God—when they sit and when they rise, when they walk, and when they work. In much the same way, God's instruction to the church is "make disciples" (Matt 28:19–20). How are these similar biblical mandates best fulfilled? In essence, the church, cooperating with the family, should co-champion spiritual formation.[160] To

---

159. Smith, "Generation to Generation," 191; Allen, "What Is Intergenerational Worship?"

160. The biblical mandate to be fruitful and multiply found in Gen 1:28 can be applied spiritually to making disciples, or spiritual formation. Likewise, the church's

do so, a primary first step should be to intentionally integrate worship. As discovered in chapter 5, intergenerational worship seeks to create opportunities that encourage spiritual formation, foster a sense of belonging, and engage all generations in worship. For intergenerational worship to fulfill the purposes listed above, planners and leaders should be intentionally focused on congregational connections.[161] I truly believe that the Scriptural foundations, the definition, and the development of intergenerational worship all culminate in the application of intentional mutuality. In the following pages, I will argue that implementing intentional mutuality in intergenerational worship will allow one generation to commend God's ways and nature to the next and will assist the church to get past being just multigenerational and experience being truly intergenerational.

WHAT IS INTENTIONAL MUTUALITY?

Holly Allen states that "for intergenerational ministry to be genuinely transformative, it needs to be more fully understood, more deeply embraced, more genuinely modeled, more intentionally facilitated, and more strategically embedded into the culture of faith communities."[162] I believe Allen is calling the church to intentionally embrace generational relationships. Because of the need to be generationally intentional in corporate worship, the lack of scholarly research in the area, and based on germinal ideas from Holly Allen and Christine Ross, I have developed the construct of intentional mutuality.[163] Corporate worship offers boundless potential for

---

mandate found in Matt 28:19–20 is also to make disciples. When the church and family co-champion spiritual formation, they work together to encourage spiritual formation, which makes disciples, thereby fulfilling their mandates.

161. Congregational interconnectedness relates to the level at which generational members are interacting with and *connecting to* members of other generations. To be truly intergenerational, a church must be interconnected so that the generations are not only in proximity to one another but are actively involved with each other—encouraging spiritual growth in each other.

162. Allen, *InterGenerate*, 23.

163. Here the authors state that "intergenerational ministry occurs when a congregation intentionally brings the generations together in mutual serving, sharing, or learning within the core activities of the church in order to live out being the body of Christ to each other and the greater community." It is from these ideas that I have developed the concept and thrust of intentional mutuality. Allen and Ross, *Intergenerational Christian Formation*, 17.

the development of intergenerational connections through the implementation of intentional mutuality in the weekly gathering.

Intentional mutuality is the purposefully designed reciprocal interaction of multiple generations within the context of corporate worship. Within this definition, we can find three specific characteristics: purposeful design, reciprocal interaction, and contextualization to worship. Following a discussion of the rationale, attributes, and implementation strategies for each of intentional mutuality's three characteristics, I will argue that intentional mutuality is the linchpin for transformation to intergenerationality.

Before we examine intentional mutuality's characteristics, there are some ideas on which we must first agree. First, to implement intentional mutuality, all generations must be present in worship. If worship is age-segregated, intergenerational worship cannot, by definition, occur. Second, the church should understand the rationale and goals behind what could seem to be a radical change in worship design. Opening communication lines between leaders and the members of the congregation will be discussed later in this chapter. Third, implementing intentional mutuality in the weekly worship gathering requires widespread willingness and support for the transition process. The senior pastor is in a key role to encourage and champion church-wide transition. With these ideas in mind, we will begin by examining the various characteristics of intentional mutuality as described by its definition: purposefully designed reciprocal interaction of multiple generations within the context of corporate worship.

Purposeful Design

God was very specific when he designed worship. As discussed previously, God initiated a revelation and response plan for worship in the garden. God further refined his worship structure at Mt. Sinai. In Exod 24, God introduced a worship design that would be used throughout the remainder of the Old Testament. God not only created a broad plan for worship, he meticulously told his children of the details concerning how worship was to be carried out. A quick reading of Exod 25 through Exod 31 reveals that God designed worship in minute detail through the intricate construction and functional design of the tabernacle and all its furnishing.

In Chronicles, God further establishes the formal structure of worship for his people through the building and consecration of the temple. The work of God in designing the temple evidences the intricate care with

What Does Being Intentional Look Like?

which God fashions worship. First, 1 Chr 28 indicates that God specifically planned worship for his people. While preparations for the building of the temple commence, David instructs his son, Solomon, on God's design for the temple. David tells Solomon that God has revealed the plan for the work of the temple: "All this he made clear to me in writing from the hand of the Lord, all the work to be done according to the plan" (1 Chr 28:19). Second, 1 Chronicles teaches that God ensures worship by his promise—David tells Solomon that God will undergird the work of the temple until its completion. The chronicler states, "Then David said to Solomon his son, 'Be strong and courageous and do it. Do not be afraid and do not be dismayed, for the Lord God, even my God, is with you. He will not leave you or forsake you, until all the work for the service of the house of the Lord is finished" (1 Chr 28:20). Third, God's all-encompassing organization of worship can be found as the ark of the covenant is brought into the newly completed temple. In 2 Chr 5, God, through the chronicler, describes the worship service that follows the installation of the ark. He describes actions of the priests, singers, instrumentalists, and the people. Fourth, God established worship through the work of his servants (1 Chr 6:1–53). The descendants of Levi became the priests of Israel. First Chronicles 6:1–30 traces the lineage of the sons of Levi: Gershon, Kohath, and Merari. God also describes the work of the musicians (1 Chr 6:31–32), and the worship work of Aaron's descendants in performing sacrifices and making atonement for the people of Israel.

In the New Testament, God continues to refine his plan for worship. In his first letter to the Corinthian church, Paul describes worship in the light of Christ's coming. Paul encourages believers to be mature in their thinking related to worship.[164] While Paul includes hymn singing and teaching in God's plan for New Testament worship, he states that Christian worship should be orderly and should edify the congregation.[165]

If worship is to build up the body of Christ, it requires clarity of thought and precise planning—for God is a God of order and not of chaos (1 Cor 14:33). If God was so specific with his design of worship in the Scripture, then modern leaders should also be intentional as they plan

---

164. "Brothers, do not be children in your thinking. Be infants in evil, but in your thinking be mature" (1 Cor 14:20).

165. "What then, brothers? When you come together, each one has a hymn, a lesson, a revelation, a tongue, or an interpretation. Let all things be done for building up" (1 Cor 14:26). "But all things should be done decently and in order" (1 Cor 14:40). See also Col 3:16.

Why Does Worshiping Intergenerationally Really Matter?

worship for God's people. To be intentional, leaders must design worship purposefully. Purposeful design encompasses four major concepts: open communication, a holistic approach, creating belongingness, and avoiding design pitfalls.

Open Communication

The first necessary aspect for transitioning to intergenerational worship and ministry is creating open lines of communication. You may be old enough to remember when the following happened. In the spring of 1985, as I was preparing to graduate from high school, the Coca Cola Company made a decision that rocked them for many years. In April of 1985, they introduced "new" Coke to much fanfare. Supposedly, the company made the move to keep up with Pepsi who had been chipping away at Coke's market share by catering to a more sophisticated taste looking for a sweeter soda. The one thing that Coca Cola didn't expect was the consumer reaction. I remember the first time I popped the top on a can of New Coke. Quite frankly, it was awful. The only thing I could think of was why did they have to go and mess up a good thing. The company doubled down and announced that they were stopping production of original Coke and moving everything to the new recipe. Cans and bottles of the original Coca Cola began flying off the shelves as people started hoarding it. By the middle of the summer, a can of original recipe Coca Cola couldn't be found anywhere. Within just a few months, the deeply apologetic company announced the return of the original recipe in its new Coca Cola Classic. All was right with the world again. The problems had happened because officials of the company and those advising them failed to communicate the full ramifications of their impending decision.

As we look toward worship, and particularly worship in an intergenerational context, opening lines of communication between leaders and attenders becomes incredibly important. Howard Vanderwell states that communication and collaboration shape success in worship planning.[166] Just like New Coke, many projects can fail from a lack of communication. Transitioning a church to a more intergenerational focus is a complex task, and communicating both the vision and the practical steps is crucial. As the church prepares to transition, the senior pastor should become the primary advocate for change. Terry York, professor of ministry at Baylor University,

---

166. Vanderwell, *Church of All Ages*, 169.

What Does Being Intentional Look Like?

contends that all aspects of the struggle must be determined early, and then couched in the form of a goal that can be readily attained.[167] The senior pastor communicates the goal through a unified vision and rationale for change. Other church staff should then support the unified vision through further communication in their ministry areas. Most churches have a mission statement that speaks of the inherent values and objectives of the church. As a part of the transition process, the mission statement may need to be adjusted to include inclusive, intergenerational language.

As the church continues to move through the transition process, open dialogue and communication are paramount.[168] Regular updates and adjustments will help the congregation stay engaged in the process. York further contends that churches need to be continually bombarded with communication that refocuses their attention on the goal. They must be reminded that what they are doing is necessary to see cross-generational worship occur.[169] Open and honest communication of goals, needs, and strategies will encourage the church—moving the process forward. But communicating is just the first step. Changing the mindset of the church must permeate every ministry and activity. It needs to span the depth and breadth of everything the church seeks to do.

Holistic Approach

When transitioning to intergenerational ministry and worship, the church's united vision should extend to every aspect of church life. Stemming from the mission statement and the pastor's vision casting, the church can begin to refocus its financial, personnel, and physical structures to match up with the new vision. It is at this point in the transition process that the theoretical ideas regarding an intergenerational transition become tangible methodologies. Financially, leaders must closely examine the church budget to ensure it will support the unified mission and vision that has been communicated. Have funds been allocated so that intergenerational ministry is highlighted? Do personnel budget items match new ministry structures?

Church personnel responsibilities may also need to be adjusted to align with the new intergenerational goals.[170] Age-oriented staff (e.g., stu-

---

167. York, "Cross-Generational Worship," 36.
168. York, "Cross-Generational Worship," 36.
169. York, "Cross-Generational Worship," 36.
170. Shirley, *Family Ministry and the Church*, 17.

Why Does Worshiping Intergenerationally Really Matter?

dent minister, children's minister, preschool minister, senior adult minister) may need to be reorganized under a single, family ministry umbrella—the reorganization may take the form of a family minister who oversees other age-focused ministers.[171] In many churches, age-group ministers function independently, seeking to further their ministry goals by focusing on making disciples of only those people in their age-specific ministry area. By realigning ministers under a single banner, the family minister can help orchestrate coordinated efforts that further connections between all the generations. Coordinated efforts can be found in unifying discipleship materials so that all generations are studying complementary lessons, streamlining ministry calendars crowded with age-segregated events to focus on events that connect the generations, and in equipping parents to fulfill their discipleship role. By doing so, the staff is better able to be unified in fulfilling the new, focused mission and purpose.

In addition to adjusting budgets and transitioning personnel, church calendars will also need to be reevaluated in response to a renewed desire to intentionally focus on intergenerational ministry. In many instances, overflowing calendars crowded with age-segregated activities can be streamlined to function more intergenerationally. Each activity of the church must be closely examined to see if it promotes generational connections. Difficult decisions may need to be made concerning long-standing ministry events that do not align with the new paradigm. In their book *Simple Church*, authors Thom Rainer and Eric Geiger offer practical suggestions for simplifying busy church calendars.[172] Rainer and Geiger suggest that, to streamline church procedures and ministries, the church must be singly focused on the unified intergenerational goal for making disciples. As a new mission statement containing intergenerational language and concepts begins to take root in the church's DNA, that statement becomes a true litmus test for all ministries and activities. Churches must compare both new and existing ministries with the intergenerational standard, and those found lacking will need to be refocused or simply retired.

While advocating for intergenerationality in worship is of primary importance in our study, a true intergenerational focus should spread beyond the sanctuary walls. It should encompass the entire church ministry. It should also move beyond the walls of the church as various generations

---

171. Strother, "Family-Equipping Ministry," 162.
172. Rainer and Geiger, *Simple Church*, 60.

do ministry together. As it does so, members can begin to feel as if they truly belong.

Creating Belongingness

Allen and Ross state, "Being intergenerational in outlook means that all generations, from toddlers to seniors, will feel welcome and included when the body of Christ gathers together; they will be intentionally received; they will belong."[173] One of the most important aspects of intergenerational worship is that it creates a sense of belongingness for everyone involved. Children, students, adults, and senior adults need to feel as if they are an important part of the congregation. They all need to feel that they have a purpose, a place, and a role to fulfill in worship. Leaders should purposefully design corporate worship times that will both *include* and *engage* all congregational members. If done correctly, the design will result in a sense of feeling at home.

There are many ways to help create a sense of belongingness. A simple way can be accomplished by including members of various generations in worship leadership positions. For example, a mother/daughter duo may greet members and guests as they come to worship, a high school senior may read the Scripture passage, a child may play a piano prelude, or a multigenerational family may lead the welcome time in the service. In each instance, using the various generations proclaims by action rather than by word that all generations are important and integral to the life of the church.

Belongingness can also be encouraged through storytelling.[174] According to Linda Staats, author and developer of HomeGrown Faith, intergenerational storytelling involves making space and giving time for telling and hearing stories from each other.[175] Storytelling can happen in many ways. As members enter the sanctuary, leaders could provide "Getting to Know You" questions on the screens or in print that will prompt intergenerational interactions. Storytelling can also occur through times of testimony. Leaders can set aside specific times during worship for either live or videotaped testimonies that share members' life stories. We can also use the written word for storytelling. Different life stories can be printed in weekly worship

---

173. Allen and Ross, *Intergenerational Christian Formation*, 198.
174. See Vanderwell, *Church of All Ages*, 96; Anthony and Anthony, *Theology for Family Ministries*, 190; and Staats, "Walking Beside Each Other," 227.
175. Staats, "Walking Beside Each Other," 227.

Why Does Worshiping Intergenerationally Really Matter?

guides, newsletters, on the church's social media accounts, and even on the church website. Storytelling seeks to involve others in living life together through understanding and knowing each other better.

A sense of belongingness can also be forged through intentionally designed elements in the worship service. A welcome time offers a unique opportunity to make all worshipers feel at home. By using members of several generations—possibly a multigenerational family—to welcome worshipers, the church models intergenerationality and everyone can sense that they belong. In much the same way, using people of various ages to lead in Scripture reading, singing, playing instruments, and prayer will help the various age groups feel that they are an important part of the community. Employing materials such as historic creeds will help to connect modern worshipers not only with each other but with generations of worshipers through the centuries.[176]

Finally, a sense of belongingness can be found as leaders intentionally plan worship music. Holly Allen contends that some degree of stylistic blending is necessary.[177] Allen further contends that while people may be musically multilingual from early childhood, certain musical styles speak their heart languages.[178] As leaders plan, they should consider the culture of their congregation and ensure that they utilize various stylistic elements that will engage the people whom they lead. Music must be theologically sound and both rhythmically and melodically singable by the congregation. Allen concludes that the songs sung by the congregation should take up residence in their hearts for their entire lives.[179] When our music speaks in our congregation's heart language, it will play over and over in their minds as they live through the week. I have been at the bedside of those who are close to death. I can tell you that it is not the sermons that come to them in those moments, it is the songs that they have sung. When we place music into the mouths of our people that deeply affects them, it will help pull them into the community of faith that is the church. It will speak across generational divides to give our people a common language in which they can worship and praise the Triune God of the universe.

---

176. Shirley states, "All those in Christ share a common inheritance and identity in the Holy Spirit; He connects all believers together from the north, south, east, and west, and joins together the saints from generations present and past." Shirley, *Family Ministry and the Church*, 19.

177. Allen, "Best Practices for Worship."

178. Allen, "Best Practices for Worship."

179. Allen, "Best Practices for Worship."

What Does Being Intentional Look Like?

Pitfalls to Avoid

When I was growing up, we didn't have the latest Atari games (I guess I am dating myself with these products). We did, however, have an Intellivision gaming system. One of my favorite games was one called Pitfall. In the game, you had to use your wits as your character, Pitfall Harry, traveled through a jungle that was littered with traps, dangerous animals, and situations requiring thought and planning to avoid. Worship in an intergenerational landscape is much the same. There are traps, dangerous animals, and situations that require careful thought and planning to navigate.

When planning for intergenerational worship, try to not be a Pitfall Harry by avoiding the following pitfalls. First, the worship planner must steer clear of decisions based on stereotypes. Hilborn and Bird caution that "one of the greatest dangers of generationally driven social and cultural analysis is the temptation to stereotype particular age groups according to their worldview in general."[180] It is a mistake to assume that a particular age group will respond in a certain fashion to different worship elements and patterns. A teen may not necessarily appreciate contemporary Christian music just as a senior adult may not gravitate stylistically to a traditional format. In my history as a worship leader, one church in which I ministered wanted to more effectively reach young adults with families. To do so, we decided adding a service that featured contemporary music and a relaxed atmosphere would attract the desired demographic. As we began the new service, we soon realized that it was being attended by primarily median and older adults. Most of the young adults remained in the blended service. There is no single stylistic method that will reach a particular age range of people. And thinking that way, can get you into trouble faster than almost anything else. As worship leaders, we should employ various styles and methods so that we can be as inclusive as possible. However, we must remain within the prevailing culture, or the DNA, of the church.

One cause for the current pattern of systemic age segregation could be traced back to decisions based on stereotypes. As in my former church described above, church leaders may have concluded that children and young families are more apt to join if a certain style or worship ethos is achieved. To that end, some churches have adjusted their musical style to attract teens and their families.[181] However, Powell, Mulder, and Griffin state that

---

180. Hilborn and Bird, *God and the Generations*, 64.
181. As a minister of music for almost thirty years, on several occasions I have been

Why Does Worshiping Intergenerationally Really Matter?

it is not a question of style that attracts emerging generations, but rather the development of relationships within the congregation.[182] While some churches may target young adults and families, stereotyping can also occur on the opposite end of the age spectrum. Other churches have developed traditional or "classic" services to retain and placate senior adults. Allen and Ross suggest that systemic age segregation in worship has resulted in "negative stereotyping and discrimination against the older population."[183] Assumptions based on stereotypes should be carefully examined before leadership acts upon them.

A second pitfall that should be avoided when purposefully designing intergenerational worship is hidden curriculum. According to Allan Harkness, hidden curriculum is implied learning that occurs from exclusions in worship.[184] For example, excluding children from participating in the Lord's Supper implies that the children are merely spectators and not participants. Leaders can alleviate this issue by creatively bringing the children along in the Supper's story and symbolism. Even though they may be barred from formal participation, the children can still feel that they are part of the corporate body and can anticipate the day they will be able to participate.[185]

In much the same way, if worship planners exclude generations from worship leadership teams (e.g., vocalists, choirs, instrumentalists, speakers, etc.), planners could be communicating that those unrepresented generations are unimportant. Likewise, texts, whether spoken or sung, that are unintelligible, difficult to read, difficult to understand, or music that is difficult to sing by all generations present may communicate that the worshipers should be mere spectators—resorting to simply watching the worship leaders perform on stage. Almost an advent of modern sacerdotalism or

---

instructed to alter worship styles or create new service types so that the church might be able to reach young families with children and students.

182. Powell et al., "Put Away the Skinny Jeans," 55.

183. Allen and Ross state, "Pervasive segregation of the elderly has yielded negative stereotyping and discrimination against the older population, which is known as ageism. They can be perceived as inflexible, depressing, less competent, passive, and senile." Allen and Ross, "Benefits of Intergenerality," 21.

184. Harkness, "Intergenerational Corporate Worship," 10.

185. Here Castleman states, "Delay is not denial. Waiting for the proper time is not idle waiting, nor is it empty. Anticipation is the best preparation for the proper moment of fulfillment. It is wise to work up a good appetite for the most significant meal in which any of us ever partake." Castleman, *Parenting in the Pew*, 126.

an expression of *ex opere operato*,[186] some modern worship services may cause attenders to simply stop participating because it may be too difficult. As a result, they become mere spectators of the worship going on up on the platform. As worship begins, the lights dim and music that could rival a major symphony orchestra or even a live rock concert could keep the worshipers from participating. Planners and leaders should be careful to plan texts and music that can be easily understood and sung, or plan instruction times to overcome difficult texts, music, and concepts. As we have already learned, worship at its core is participatory—worship is our response to the revelation of God.

Much like hidden curriculum, tokenism is another pitfall resulting from implied learning. In many instances, when a church seeks to be more intergenerational, they find ways to incorporate multiple age groups in worship. However, if done without forethought and intentional design, the practice can cause more harm than good. For example, Harkness suggests a worship planner may seek intergenerationality by simply incorporating children into the worship plans.[187] An easy way to accomplish this goal is by using a children's choir to present a song during the corporate worship service. The children learn the song in an age-segregated rehearsal. The children then *perform* the song, which may be completely "unrelated to the thematic or structural flow of the service."[188] In effect, the church has communicated to the children that they are just performers—a thought further made much worse by typical adult reactions to the *performance*. Howard Vanderwell states:

> When our responses signal to them [children leading worship] that we expect them to be "cute" rather than an intrinsic part of the drama of worship, we may have missed their contribution to the dialogue between God and God's people. Our responses to what we perceive as "cuteness" may seem appropriate at the time but may cheapen their contributions and miss the point entirely. Our children are never "merely cute." They are taking their place in deeply and profoundly telling the glorious story of salvation.[189]

---

186. Sacerdotalism describes the separation of the laity and clergy in which the people are distanced from the work of worship. In much the same way, *ex opere operato*, Latin for "from the work worked," describes the imparting of grace through just the observation of the sacramental acts of worship.

187. Harkness, "Intergenerational Corporate Worship," 18n.

188. Harkness, "Intergenerational Corporate Worship," 18n.

189. Vanderwell, *Church of All Ages*, 183. See also chapter 11 for creative ways to

Why Does Worshiping Intergenerationally Really Matter?

The church's children are not seeking to perform, they are seeking to lead their mothers and fathers, their sisters and brothers in worship. When leadership is mistaken for performance, the church begins to drive home the notion that worship equates to performance. Therefore, following *their* performance, the children might then be excused to go back to *their* worship service in children's church, or just to sit with their parents and behave for the rest of the service. To avoid tokenism, the worship planner must use creativity to integrate all age groups so that they become an essential part of the fabric of the service.

In a fourth pitfall, Kara Powell, Jake Mulder, and Brad Griffin identify eight unnecessary qualities for churches seeking to attract emerging generations and their families.[190] Careful planners of intergenerational worship must understand that purposeful design moves past surface issues of style to elements of substance. Powell, Mulder, and Griffin's eight unnecessary qualities include: a trendy location, a specific denomination, culturally relevant pastoral teaching style and dress, a precise size, an exact target age, a big budget, a contemporary worship style, and a big modern building. Each of these qualities merely engage surface issues. However, purposeful design involves opening lines of communication and presenting a holistic approach that moves beyond the superficial to create a sense of belongingness and mutual serving and learning that is reciprocated among all worship participants.

RECIPROCAL INTERACTION

Intergenerational worship must also include reciprocity. Reciprocity is defined as a *mutual* exchange between persons.[191] Reciprocal relationships—relationships that express mutuality, or a bidirectional exchange of ideas, knowledge, and commitments—are necessary for spiritual formation in intergenerational worship.[192] Reciprocity can be found in three aspects of intergenerational worship: it is biblical, it is relational, and it encourages spiritual formation.

---

introduce preschool and children's choirs in worship.

190. Powell et al., "Put Away the Skinny Jeans," 55.

191. Merriam-Webster, "Reciprocity."

192. Richards states, "To enable enduring faith to develop, we need intergenerational contexts and relationships. Otherwise, we only have a sense of how to be Christian at our stage of life and faith." Richards, "Walking Together," 31.

Reciprocity Is Biblical

The concept of reciprocity in generational relationships is found throughout Scripture. In Acts 20:7–12, the apostle Paul was gathered with the church in Troas. The church had come to celebrate the Lord's Supper together before Paul was to leave in the morning. Paul, taking advantage of every moment, continued to preach well after midnight. At some point in the evening, Eutychus, a young man, found a perch high in a window from which he could hear Paul. As evening became night, Eutychus had trouble staying awake. Falling into a deep sleep, he slipped from the window and fell multiple stories to his death. Paul and the others gathered that night ran to the dead youth. Paul threw himself upon the youth and proclaimed him to be alive. Eutychus, then very much alive, was taken away and the congregation returned to the upper room to eat the meal. The story of Eutychus and Paul sheds some valuable insight on the intergenerationality of New Testament worship. First, the young man was present during worship. He came to hear Paul and learn from his teaching. Eutychus came to participate in worship. Second, through his ordeal, Eutychus also encouraged both the body of Christ and Paul. The story of Eutychus's death and subsequent resurrection gave a poignant reminder of God's power to the church who had gathered to celebrate Christ's death and resurrection.[193]

The very nature of God's design for worship is reciprocal. God reveals himself and man responds. In the same way, the model of reciprocity could be further extended to worshiping generations. God calls the people to worship, and they all respond. Allan Harkness remarks, "Just as Hebrew children participated in the worship rituals and festivals of their people, so children were present and participated with adults in the corporate worship events of the New Testament churches."[194] In response, an early step toward intergenerationality would be to bring all of God's people, young and old, together in worship so that they might follow biblical principles and interact relationally.

Reciprocity Is Relational

Reciprocity requires a bidirectional response from two or more parties. In legal terms, reciprocity grants an individual the same rights and privileges

---

193. White, *Intergenerational Religious Education*, 69.
194. Harkness, "Intergenerational Corporate Worship," 13.

as those granted by another authority. In other words, if a person has been issued a license to drive a motor vehicle in one state, he has the right to drive in all other states in the Union. Reciprocity works relationally—there is give and take between two parties. A person can drive in multiple states, yet he must follow the driving laws specific to each separate state. If I'm driving the speed limit of seventy-five miles per hour and I cross the border with a state where the maximum speed is sixty-five miles per hour, I am required to follow the new state's mandated limits. If not, I am subject to the consequences of breaking the law.

Within intergenerational ministries and worship, reciprocity functions as members, under God's authority and direction, express themselves in relationship with those of other generations. However, as Csinos and Beckwith contend, "proximity does not necessarily equate with integration."[195] Just because there are multiple generations present does not mean that there is reciprocity. Reciprocity only occurs as multiple generational members interact, and a sense of equality or community is formed.[196] The sense of equality/community is further encouraged by an "openness to being changed through the relationship with the other."[197] Many times older members are presumed upon to change for the sake of attracting a younger audience. However, both old and young must be willing to accommodate change for the sake of the gospel. According to Terry York, the church must realize that reciprocity in intergenerational worship is bidirectional.[198] Reciprocity in intergenerational worship must move in both directions: old to young and young to old. As older generations may be asked to sing modern worship songs for the sake of children and students, so too must students and children be willing to move beyond simple preferences and seek to participate as heartily in singing traditional hymns as they do songs from the latest worship bands.

Accommodating reciprocal relationships in intergenerational worship can be both simple and complex. A church can simply add members of multiple generations to worship leadership teams. The teams (vocal, choral, and instrumental) that lead worship each Sunday should be a fair

195. Csinos and Beckwith, "Better Together," 36.
196. Harkness states that interpersonal interactions occurring cross-generationally reach the level of intergenerationality only when a "sense of mutuality and equality is encouraged between the participants." Harkness, "Intergenerational and Homogeneous-Age Education," 52.
197. Allen, *InterGenerate*, 18.
198. York, "Cross-Generational Worship," 40.

What Does Being Intentional Look Like?

representation of the composition of the whole congregation. Including various generations in leadership also opens doors for mentorship opportunities as more experienced leaders and musicians instruct and encourage burgeoning musicians. Adding children, students, and senior adults to worship leadership teams and instrumental ensembles is a simple way to promote reciprocity in generational relationships that also encourages belongingness.

Mentorships can extend beyond the Sunday morning platform. Proficient adult musicians can mentor future leaders and musicians. Assigning adults in one-to-one or one-to-two mentoring relationships with kids in the children's choir, student music program members, or beginning instrumentalists brings another adult role model into the life of a child as they seek to co-champion the efforts of the parents in discipleship.

In worship service planning and leadership, relational reciprocity can be forged by including various generational members on the intergenerational worship planning team. It can also be encouraged by using pairings from different generations to lead specific elements in the corporate worship time. A parent/child or grandparent/grandchild duo can welcome guests and help children, students, and adults feel as though they belong. Members from different generations can also be used to lead in Scripture readings, creeds, or other spoken words during the service. Various generational members could also bring new life and impetus to times of sharing body needs and opportunities (what we lovingly call the ministry of announcements). Intergenerational groups can also lead in prayer, times of corporate confession, and in assisting with the offering. In each instance, the reciprocal relationships from multiple generations will encourage and strengthen intergenerational bonds across the congregation. All of these activities will help remind the congregation of the unified vision and mission to be intergenerational weekly.

Reciprocity Encourages Spiritual Formation

As we discussed earlier, intergenerational connections aid in spiritual formation. As generations interact—one man, one woman, one child—Prov 27:17 tells us that each spurs spiritual growth in the others. Csinos and Beckwith state, "Young people benefit from relationships with nonparent adults, with older friends, mentors, teachers, youth leaders, and other adults who walk with them on the journey that is life."[199] Likewise, the apostle Paul utilized intergenerational mentoring relationships with Timothy, Titus, Philemon, and Onesimus to further the cause of the gospel.[200] Allen and Ross posit, "Frequent cross-generational experiences are essential to Christian formation and the development of mature faith . . . further, we are convinced that *perennially* segregating the various generations inherently hinders spiritual growth and development."[201] In other words, intergenerational connections are essential in spiritual formation—so much so that it forms the thesis for their book *Intergenerational Christian Formation*.[202] Norma deWaal Malefyt and Howard Vanderwell insist that intergenerational connections are required for spiritual formation.[203] Likewise, John Roberto proclaims what we have already seen in Scripture: from the first days of the church, spiritual formation through intergenerational connections is essential.[204] Over and over, the experts tell us that spiritual formation is both encouraged and precipitated by intergenerational connections and experience. If the church is to fulfill its mission to make disciples (Matt 28:19–20), then it should make the most of intergenerational relationships.

While we cannot truly underestimate the importance of intergenerational connections, there is also benefit in utilizing some age-oriented or age-segregated ministry. We have already learned that John Roberto encourages the church to find a balance between segregation and integration of the generations. Hear what Roberto says:

> Age-specific and intergenerational faith formation are not either-or choices; they are complementary. Lifelong faith formation balances age-specific and intergenerational programs, activities, and strategies. Throughout the life cycle there is a need for age-specific groups (and interest-centered groups) to gather because of age-related differences in development and age-related learning

---

199. Csinos and Beckwith, "Better Together," 34.

200. Timothy (1 Cor 4:17; 2 Tim 1:2), Titus (Titus 1:4), Philemon (Phlm 1), and Onesimus (Phlm 10).

201. Allen and Ross, *Intergenerational Christian Formation*, 25.

202. The thesis of *Intergenerational Christian Formation* might be summed up by the statement, "A cross-generational group of believing people uniquely fosters healthy spiritual growth and development among its constituents." Allen and Ross, *Intergenerational Christian Formation*, 23.

203. Malefyt and Vanderwell, "Reaching All Generations in Worship," 12.

204. Roberto, "Our Future Is Intergenerational," 106.

needs. Each congregation needs to determine the balance that is appropriate.[205]

Roberto is telling us that there is still a need for some age-specific groups in our churches. We can address issues that are directly related to various generations in small groups focused on those generations. For example, a church can create a small group that equips young adults to be godly parents. Likewise, a group of toddlers can best learn about the love of God through physical, concrete activities rather than a heady discipleship time. The key is to create a balance between age segregation and age integration. Find moments each week when you can intensely and intentionally focus on creating connections between the generations. Even coordinating Bible study topics in age-segregated classes will allow parents to connect with their children. They will be able to expound upon what their children and students have learned—digging deeper and making applications to their particular real-life situations. When age-segregated ministries co-champion intergenerational ministry, reciprocity is encouraged. Therefore, reciprocity that happens biblically and relationally aids in spiritual formation.

BRINGING IT ALL TOGETHER: CONTEXTUALIZATION TO WORSHIP

As the dawn of the twenty-first century approached, some ministry leaders began to see that all was not well in the church. What God had designed to be intergenerational had strayed far from his initial plan. Therefore, those leaders began to devise ways to bring the generations back together. However, as we have seen, those churches seeking to reconnect the various generations did so without much forethought in worship. As a result, those planning and leading worship sought ways to bring the generations back together and a brand-new multigenerational worship concept emerged.

As a result of the multigen focus, composers and music publishers embraced the idea and began to create multigenerational worship resources. However, as they did so, few attempts really rose to the level of being truly intergenerational. Most products simply encouraged using younger soloists, readers, or children/student choirs to accompany the adult choir. Each group would rehearse their individual parts in age-segregated rehearsals

---

205. Roberto, "Our Future Is Intergenerational," 110.

Why Does Worshiping Intergenerationally Really Matter?

and the ensembles were brought together at the last moment to rehearse and perform. Following the performance, the individual children, students, and adults went their separate ways until another worship service featuring a multigenerational moment was planned. The process yielded little time for intergenerational connections to form and flourish, and very little room for connections between the generations to blossom into spiritual formation.

As we have seen, God placed the mandate of spiritual formation on both the family *and* the church. Working together, the family and church can co-champion discipleship and fulfill their mandates. I also firmly believe that God's discipleship mandate extends to worship. Allan Harkness contends that "the edificatory potential of corporate worship events is widely documented, and in this respect, they can be considered to be a significant learning experience."[206] Biblical worship forms the believer. The historical concept of *lex orandi, lex credendi*[207] reiterates worship's formational nature—the law of prayer (religion) and the law of belief (liturgy) interact to form us spiritually. Let's take a closer look (see figure 7.1).

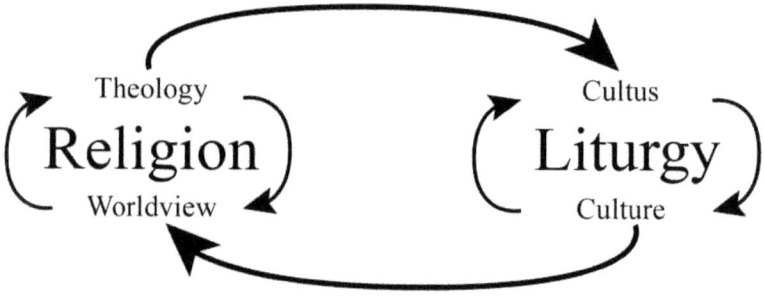

Figure 7.1. The relationship of religion and liturgy[208]

Our religion is made up of two different aspects. First, our religion is formed by our worldview—how we innately and unconsciously view the world around us. Second, it is also influenced by our theology, or our

206. Harkness, "Intergenerational Corporate Worship," 9.

207. *Lex orandi* (law of what is prayed), *lex credendi* (law of what is believed) is a circular construct that speaks of how a believer's religion (consisting of the relationship between worldview and theology) affects or informs his liturgy (consisting of the relationship between his culture and cultus). The cyclical nature of *lex orandi, lex credendi* speaks to the formational nature of worship.

208. Aniol, "Introduction."

What Does Being Intentional Look Like?

reasoned, conscious response to the world. In much the same way, our liturgy—the way we worship—is also formed and influenced by two different aspects. Our culture is the world around us, the community of people with whom we live, and who exert influence upon us. Culture can be described as the way a certain people group live. On the other hand, cultus has a more narrow view. Cultus describes the way a certain people worship. Denominations have a certain cultus. Catholics worship one way while a Southern Baptist service will look completely different. Even within denominations, each church will have a unique cultus all its own. The culture and cultus work together to form our views and liturgical practice.

There is also a macro effect. The believer's religion informs his liturgy which in turn informs his religion. Liturgy then forms the religion of the believer just as religion in turn informs the liturgy. If that formation occurs within an age-segregated vacuum, the biblical benefits of intergenerational spiritual formation are unrealized. However, if worship is intentionally designed with intergenerational connections in mind, the generations can experience its full weight. If worship is spiritually formational, how much more formative could it be if done biblically in an intentional intergenerational relationship context?

As we saw in part one, the biblical concepts of intergenerationality in worship go far beyond the modern church's latest multigen worship attempts described above. God created both the family (Ps 145:4) and the church (Matt 28:19–20) to make disciples of *all* peoples. To fulfill this mission the church would be better served by returning to biblical intergenerationality—especially within the corporate worship context. Allan Harkness believes that intergenerational worship "has the potential to enhance the spiritual enrichment and faith development of others by virtue of the mutual contributions the range of generational groups can offer."[209] Corporate worship can deepen all the worshipers' spiritual formation if it is planned and led while intentionally focusing on intergenerational connections.

In this chapter, we have discovered what being intergenerational truly looks like. We have seen that the attempts that many churches are making do not truly move beyond simple multigenerationality. We also learned that implementing intentional mutuality when planning and leading worship may help to foster spiritual connections through *being purposeful* and creating an environment where *reciprocity* between the various generations can bloom and grow into significant spiritual formation for *all* the

---

209. Harkness, "Intergenerational Corporate Worship," 15.

Why Does Worshiping Intergenerationally Really Matter?

worshipers in our churches. In the next chapter, we will focus on specific ways we can use to foster intergenerational connections in our weekly worship gatherings.

Questions for Thought and Discussion

1. Are we being intentional as we seek to bring the generations together in worship?
2. Does our plan extend to all other aspects of the church or are there ministry silos that still need to be breached?
3. Do church attenders of all ages feel a sense of belonging in our services and in our other ministries? Are we encouraging or inhibiting belonging by the way we "do" worship?
4. Is there reciprocity in our services? Are the generations learning from each other? Are they being spiritually formed by each other? Why or why not?
5. Are we stuck in the endless cycle of planning for specific multigen services, or are we intentionally planning for intergenerational involvement in every service?

8

Making the Big Shift
Reviving God's Plan for Worship

> Intergenerational worship is corporate worship in which leaders seek to create opportunities that encourage spiritual formation and foster a sense of belonging as all generations engage in the pattern of revelation and response established by God.

As we look at our working definition of intergenerational worship above, we can isolate four major characteristics: create opportunities, encourage spiritual formation, foster a sense of belonging, and engage all generations in worship. The ways in which we put these four characteristics to work will help to form a persuasive motivation for change in the modern church.

Create Opportunities

The first characteristic of intergenerational worship is probably the simplest to enact. Intentionally designed intergenerational worship should create opportunities through which relationships across multiple generations can be formed. Allen and Ross have called these cross-generational moments *interconnecting*—creating meaningful ties with older or younger believers.[210]

---

210. Allen and Ross state that a "fundamental aspect of spiritual development is *interconnecting*, that is, linking oneself to narratives, communities, mentors, beliefs,

Why Does Worshiping Intergenerationally Really Matter?

As senior adults, young adults, students, and children worship together, they can connect and interact together—learning from one another.

Leaders who plan worship with intergenerationality in mind seek to find space for cross-generational interaction. As worshipers sing together, as they read Scripture together, as they focus on hearing the message, as they participate in the Lord's Supper together, they begin to understand one another and thus can begin to develop deeper relationships. Parents and grandparents can assist children in following Scripture while it is being read. Students can be taught what it means to serve the church and others by older mentors through helping with an offertory or greeting members as they arrive. Young parents might be assisted in teaching their children to worship by "adopted" grandparents.

But the reverse is also true. Age-segregated worship, by its very nature, does not allow for these multigenerational connections. For an age-oriented, multigenerational church seeking to become more intergenerational, we must first bring the generations together in worship. They need to be in the same space at the same time. They need to see each other across the room. They need to breathe the same air, and they need to participate in worship *together!*

Encourage Spiritual Formation

Second, intergenerational worship should encourage spiritual formation. As we have discussed earlier, intergenerational interaction aids in spiritual development. The apostle Paul speaks of mentoring relationships in Titus 2:1–8. Paul specifically references intergenerational relationships as he speaks of older men with younger men and older women with younger women. In each case, the older participant is to pass down wisdom gained through life experiences and godly learning. Expounding on concepts Paul introduces in Titus 2, Gordon Smith contends,

> The witness of the Scriptures and of virtually every human culture suggests that one of the most pivotal and thus crucial dimensions of human formation, and thus spiritual formation, is the inter-generational dynamic: older men with younger men; older women passing on the faith to younger women. One generation

---

traditions, and/or practices that remain significant over time." Allen and Ross, *Intergenerational Christian Formation*, 63.

encouraging, blessing, and transmitting wisdom to the next generation.[211]

Smith reiterates that spiritual formation happens within the context of intergenerational relationships. Using social science, David Csinos and Ivy Beckwith, proponents of the age-integrated church, adopt Vygotsky's zone of proximal development to describe the benefits of spiritual mentoring.[212] The zone of proximal development measures the difference in what someone with no abilities can learn before a mentor steps in to guide them. Applying the zone of proximal development to spiritual formation, Csinos and Beckwith state, "As children engage in tasks and activities with people who are older and more experienced than them, their learning is enhanced and their formation is spurred forward."[213]

Let's take these ideas of mentoring and put them into practice in worship. For example, when worship leaders plan the Lord's Supper, they should allow time for parents to instruct their young children. In doing so, the child is engaged in the service and is spiritually nurtured even though the child does not formally participate. There are specific ways to encourage parents to teach their children about the Lord's Supper in chapter 11. Likewise, as a parent who understands the benefit of a daily time of personal worship instructs their child, that child's understanding and practice of worship is expanded. In the same way, as a loving grandparent shows a parent how to discipline their children in worship, the parent matures spiritually. The process of mentoring furthers spiritual development.

Csinos and Beckwith further argue that mentoring also has bidirectional benefits. They claim that just as children learn from adults, those same adults can and will learn from the knowledge and the experiences of the young people.[214] James W. White also suggests that adults can be encouraged to worship by the excitement of children. He states that "adults learn from youngsters, as when a child gets up on tip-toe to see a baptism—thus suggesting to nearby adults that 'something wonderful' is happening,

---

211. Smith, "Generation to Generation," 182.

212. Lev Vygotsky (1896–1934) defined the zone of proximal development as the difference between what a learner currently understands and can accomplish without help and what a learner does not currently understand but can accomplish with help from a guide/mentor. When applied to spiritual formation, Csinos and Beckwith contend that children learn best when someone older and more experienced can help guide them in the process. Vygotsky, *Mind in Society*, 86.

213. Csinos and Beckwith, "Better Together," 35.

214. Csinos and Beckwith, "Better Together," 35.

causing those adults to look again."[215] Worship leaders should plan for moments that children can instruct and inspire adults: video testimonies of life-transformation at a summer camp or Vacation Bible School, a group of children reading Scripture, or musical worship led by a children's choir or student worship team that ties into the structure and substance of the service.

Some of the most moving services we have experienced in our church are when our students or children lead us. Several times a year, our adults step back from leadership and allow the emerging generations to lead all of us in worship for a full service. We had our annual staff planning retreat yesterday looking forward to the next calendar year. As we were doing so, we planned specific times that our children and students would take the lead in our services. During that conversation, our student pastor talked about one of his greatest pet peeves in ministry: people calling the students "the church of tomorrow." I wholeheartedly share his opinion. We adults must come to understand this foundational principle: the emerging generations are not the church of tomorrow; they are the church of today! When we push their leadership off for a time when they are more "spiritually mature" or better equipped to lead, we hamper both their spiritual growth and the spiritual formation of the whole body. We can learn so much about God's love, his compassion, his mercy, his grace, and his salvation when we allow the emerging generations an opportunity to lead with passion, excitement, and spiritual fervor. Is their leadership perfect? No. I have a child who will always add his own choreography to a song if I haven't created movement for everyone. But his passion for worship inspires and challenges my own leadership. How long has it been since I have allowed God total control over my mind and body as I lead in worship? When the emerging generations lead, it may never be perfect, but it is perfectly following God's plan for worship because it edifies the body and forms us spiritually.

Support for mentoring relationships can also be found in Scripture. The apostle Paul offers a biblical model whereby he mentors younger men in the faith. Throughout his epistles, Paul describes mentoring relationships he has with younger believers, or his "sons" in the faith: Timothy, Titus, Philemon, and Onesimus.[216] As mentor and mentee interact, they encourage spiritual growth and development in the other.

---

215. White, *Intergenerational Religious Education*, 48.

216. Timothy (1 Cor 4:17; 2 Tim 1:2), Titus (Titus 1:4), Philemon (Phlm 1), and Onesimus (Phlm 10).

The mentoring relationships we create within our worship services are crucial. Whether it is our children and students mentoring the adults through their leadership or just their fervor and enthusiasm, or intentional mentoring from the adults to the emerging generations, those relationships are crucial in building intergenerational connections.

Foster Belongingness

Third, intergenerational worship should help to foster a sense of belonging among all participants. In Maslow's hierarchy of needs, a sense of belongingness falls only behind physiological and safety needs (see figure 8.1).[217] Maslow states that man "will hunger for affectionate relations with people in general, namely, for a place in his group, and he will strive with great intensity to achieve this goal."[218] Therefore, the need to belong is a high priority for man. As intergenerational relationships are strengthened, a sense of community is achieved, and belongingness is deepened.[219]

Figure 8.1. Maslow's hierarchy of needs

Both children and adults can feel at home as they are welcomed to fully participate in all aspects of worship. Worship leaders can plan specific

217. Maslow, *Theory of Human Motivation*, 17.
218. Maslow further states that "he will want to attain such a place more than anything else in the world and may even forget that once, when he was hungry, he sneered at love." Maslow, *Theory of Human Motivation*, 17.
219. Allen, "Best Practices for Worship."

Why Does Worshiping Intergenerationally Really Matter?

elements of worship that purposefully include all generations: singing songs that students are learning in their age-segregated times, inviting an older child to lead in the reading of Scripture, inviting a young musician to play a prelude or offertory, incorporating a children's sermon that is intently focused on connecting the children to the fabric of the service, encouraging older adults to adopt a young family in worship and sit with them. Each of these worship elements helps to connect the various generations to the process of worship and thus to each other. However, community and belonging can also be interrupted when a church disenfranchises age segments from certain worship activities and elements.

Lance Armstrong, Uniting Church minister and former Australian Parliament member, contends that when children are dismissed from corporate worship halfway through the service, the church communicates that the children do not truly belong. He states, "This practice fails to give the children a feeling of belonging. Rather, it is saying to the children, 'We will tolerate you for so long, but then we want you to go so that we can get on with the real worship.'"[220] For some churches, the practice of dismissing children to a segregated worship time began to compensate for development and attention span issues. In most cases, churches actually underestimate the attention span and comprehension of children in the pew. Children will glean more than leaders expect when remaining in the main service.[221]

Many churches also inadvertently communicate to children that they are merely spectators and not true participants. When pastors and other staff plan a children's sermon as a part of corporate worship, they often simply use the children as props as they speak to the adults. In a service I recently attended, the children gathered on the platform steps with the pastor. As the congregation continued to sing, the pastor spoke and interacted with the children as they arrived at the platform. However, when the time for the children's sermon began, the pastor stood and spoke directly to those people remaining in the pews. The children were suddenly left staring at the pastor's knees and were completely disconnected from the service—they had their moment with the pastor, but then he moved on to speak to the adults in the room. In essence, the children had become an

---

220. Armstrong, *Children in Worship*, 16.

221. White states that much of what children learn in worship is "caught" rather than "taught." As children participate in worship, other people model how a worshiper should act and what a worshiper should do. Children can come to understand their role as a worshiper through simply watching others worship. White, *Intergenerational Religious Education*, 78.

illustration for the pastor to use—a token. If, however, the pastor had remained on their level physically and taught *them*, the children would have been better prepared to receive what the pastor later delivered in his message, applying it to their spiritual lives. The remainder of the congregation would have also learned from the same lesson. Diana Garland concurs that in the child's estimation, in instances like the one detailed above, the children "have had their five minutes of worship, and then either return to their parents in the pew or exit pulpit left to go to children's church."[222] In one of my favorite analogies, Garland further states that many times, children are given "'ecclesiastical happy meals' . . . that contain crayons and pictures to color, a snack and sometimes a picture book—designed to entertain children and keep them quiet."[223] In my current church, the children's minister creates a weekly worship handout specifically for the children. The handout is directly linked to the content of the service. It includes notes from the pastor's sermon, a place for thoughts related to the music that was sung, and coloring pictures and activities that relate thematically to that day's service. Instead of busywork to keep the children occupied, the children are engaged in the essential structure of the service—they are actively listening and participating. When the service concludes, the children can find the pastor, show him their completed handout, and they will receive a little piece of candy as a reward. It's not the reward of candy that is important, but the connection with the pastor that yields the greatest reward. Unless leaders exercise special care and tailor the materials to that day's specific service elements, the children are excluded from active participation and their sense of belonging is seriously undermined.

The amount of information that children can learn in a worship service is also often underestimated by leaders. Scott T. Brown states that "children get something out of everything they experience. That is why there is great value, even for an infant, to experience authentic worship in the meeting of God's people."[224] Even infants can experience the loving embrace of a parent as they perceive the undulating rhythms and patterns of worship. I have often expressed that I was active in the church beginning nine months before I was born. My parents immersed me in the cultus and rhythm of worship from the very beginning, and therefore, that rhythm has become a natural part of life.

222. Garland, *Family Ministry*, 452.
223. Garland, *Family Ministry*, 452–53.
224. Brown, *A Weed in the Church*, 62.

Why Does Worshiping Intergenerationally Really Matter?

In much the same way, older worshipers must also find a sense of belonging. As many churches seek relevance in the culture, they do so at the expense of senior adults. Churches may drastically change the musical style, liturgical format, and long-standing church traditions in the quest to attract young families. In "One Congregation's Story," Stan Mast argues against adaptation, stating a church needs only to develop a "churchwide mindset that places a passion for God at the center of worship."[225] The passion a church exhibits will encourage all generational members. For all of God's children to sense they belong in worship, leaders must consider elements that are inclusive, instructive, and participatory.

Encourage Worship Participation

Finally, intergenerational worship also encourages engagement and participation in worship. As we've discussed in part two, God designed worship to be participatory—as God reveals himself, man responds. True intergenerational worship gives participants of every age some space to respond to God's revelation. Allen and Ross state that churches must bring generations together to serve, share, and learn with each other.[226] How can preschoolers and senior adults both participate in the same service? A creative worship leader will plan elements of worship that engage all generations. For example, incorporating music of varying styles that can be sung easily by all ages will help to engage them. Engaging senior adults could be as simple as providing large-print hymnals and Bibles. Allowing time for specific, age-appropriate responses—thematic coloring pages for preschoolers, creating times of corporate confession, and directed prayer times for students and adults—further strengthens the responsorial nature of worship and encourages participation. Stan Mast suggests giving children, students, adults, and senior adults an opportunity for controlled feedback following services will also help to create a sense of belonging resulting in greater engagement.[227]

---

225. Here, adaptation refers to a church making changes to target a specific generation. In other words, a church may change its musical style or liturgical structures to reach students and young families. In doing so, the church could alienate older generations. However, if the change occurs not on the superficial level of structures, but on congregational mindset, those same changes to liturgical structure or musical style will be overridden by an overwhelming desire to see all generations reached. Mast, "One Congregation's Story," 144.

226. Allen and Ross, *Intergenerational Christian Formation*, 17.

227. Mast describes a plan that engages various generations at four separate points in

Making the Big Shift

Intergenerational worship must move beyond a multigenerational mindset that simply recognizes other generations exist. True intergenerational worship calls for participatory responses in worship. We must plan ways in which members of every generation can actively participate in worship. Creativity in worship planning can occur in many different ways, and we will discuss some examples thoroughly in part three. Planning and leading specific worship elements must involve a conscious effort to include all generations. A hallmark of intergenerational worship, intentional mutuality offers tangible ways to be inclusive in our corporate worship. In the next several chapters, we will discuss ways to implement intentional mutuality in the worship planning and leading process.

CONCLUDING THOUGHTS

Diana Garland has stated that age-segregated worship "tears at the fabric of families."[228] Garland's view is supported by Scripture. The Bible details that God designed worship to be carried out and experienced in the midst of an intergenerational community. As the church has broken away from the biblical intent and design of worship, it has suffered some dire consequences. In a 2018 research study, LifeWay Research determined that 66 percent of students who were active church participants in their high school years became inactive between age eighteen and twenty-two.[229] While the causation for this startling statistic cannot be overwhelmingly attributed to age-segregated worship, there are telltale signs of its being a factor. As noted earlier, intergenerational worship provides for a sense of belonging and engagement in the body of Christ through worship. Without that belonging, emerging adults disengage from the church—a structure they view as irrelevant and distant.[230]

Ben Trueblood, the author of LifeWay's study, later states that making intergenerational connections with adults was a key in students' church participation following high school. Trueblood cites the following statistics:

> 88% of students with no intergenerational connections dropped out.

---

the planning and execution of a worship service: in preparation, in the pew, up front, and afterward. Mast, "One Congregation's Story," 137–140.

228. Garland, *Family Ministry*, 451.
229. Trueblood, *Within Reach*, 12.
230. Trueblood, *Within Reach*, 115.

Why Does Worshiping Intergenerationally Really Matter?

72% of students with one or two intergenerational connections dropped out.

58% of students with three or more intergenerational connections dropped out.[231]

From these statistics, Trueblood extrapolates, "The more adults investing in an individual student's life, the less likely the student is to walk away from church after graduation."[232] John Roberto further asserts that the reason teenagers leave the church is that the church never properly introduced themselves to the teens.[233] Since many teens have only participated in age-segregated ministries—discipleship, missions, and worship—they have never had the opportunity to form intergenerational relationships outside those ministries. In effect, Roberto believes that these teens have never truly been a part of the church—but rather just a subsidiary member. However, when properly planned and executed, intergenerational worship creates opportunities for intergenerational connections that can bring about a sense of belongingness and engagement.

Intentionally designed intergenerational worship also fosters spiritual development. Scripture states in Prov 27:17, "One man sharpens another." God created man to live in community. From the beginning God said that it was not good for man to be alone (Gen 2:18), so he instituted the family. The overwhelming evidence of Scripture calls for the family to be the primary source of spiritual formation (Gen 1:28; 9:8–9; 17:1–14; 22:17–18; Exod 12:26–27; Deut 4:9–10; 6:1–9; 11:18–19; 2 Chr 20:13; Ps 48; 78; 79; 145; 148; Joel 1:1–3; Acts 16:14–15, 30–37; 18:8; Eph 5:22—6:9; Col 3:18–25; 2 Tim 1:1–7; Titus 2). The church should partner with the family to become a co-champion of the children's spiritual development. To do so, intergenerational corporate worship provides a means for equipping and a resource for developing further intergenerational connections for both parent and child.

Developing a biblical rationale and plan for intergenerational worship is important as the church continues to develop. The plan, however, cannot be a haphazard application of principles derived from various sources. To lead intergenerational worship effectively, there must be a systematic

---

231. Trueblood, *Within Reach*, 27.
232. Trueblood, *Within Reach*, 27.
233. Roberto, "Our Future Is Intergenerational," 110.

approach to planning, and those systems can be found in implementing intentional mutuality.

Questions for Thought and Discussion

1. Where does my church/ministry fall on the spectrum of intergenerationality? Are we segregated?
2. What are some of the things that we are doing now that could be truly intergenerational with only a few tweaks?
3. What are some of the things/ministries that we are doing now that are hampering us in becoming intergenerational?
4. Is my church/ministry willing to make the big shift to becoming more intergenerational in focus?
5. Are we creating opportunities for intergenerational connections? If not, what can we do to start?
6. How is my church/ministry making everyone from every generation feel like they belong and are at home?
7. Are we actively and intentionally focusing on creating intergenerational connections that can lead to spiritual formation?

PART THREE

How Can I Be Intentionally Intergenerational in Worship?

9

Planning for Intergenerational Worship

A FEW YEARS AGO, my pastor and I sat in his office one Monday afternoon and agonized about the worship life of our church. Everything in the church was good. The church was multigenerational and located in a small but growing city. Giving was up. Attendance was edging upward. We were baptizing new believers. Complaining was at an all-time low. Yet, there was something not quite right. We both sensed a catch in our spirits. After some long discussions, we determined that we had become stale, stagnant, and everything we did came from a sense of fulfilling the status quo and not upsetting the apple cart. When things are good, it is so very hard to see what is truly missing. What we finally realized was that we lacked intentionality in what we were doing. This revelation soon sparked an idea that began to change the nature and structure of what we were doing in worship.

A Spark of Creativity

We determined from that meeting, and other subsequent times together, that *we* were doing all the planning for worship. *We* were pouring through Scripture, music, drama, video, and other resources, trying to come up with a plan that would encourage all our people in our corporate times of worship. *We* had spent our creativity and were sorely lacking in new and fresh ideas that would help to connect members of every generation in worship. Something had to change. In those moments, we decided to form a Creative Worship Task Force.

How Can I Be Intentionally Intergenerational in Worship?

A Creative Worship Task Force (CWTF) is just what it sounds like: a group of church members tasked with the goal of finding creatively intentional ways to connect all the generations in our church through our weekly worship gatherings. We decided to form this group using active worshipers from every generation. We incorporated older children, students, young adults, median adults, and senior adults—every generation would have a voice. Their job was a simple one, yet it was a long labor of love that would stretch out for years and impact the format of our worship services.

The CWTF had a written purpose statement that summed up their task. The purpose statement was included in every correspondence, on every meeting agenda, and was voiced at every opportunity:

> The Creative Worship Task Force exists to enhance, plan, coordinate, evaluate, and encourage the body's time of corporate worship with special attention given to intergenerational involvement.

From this simple mandate, the team sought to find ways we could intentionally connect members of all generations. Even before I had seriously studied what would become intentional mutuality, we were putting those very principles into practice.

Creating the Team

As with all teams, one of the most important steps—one that will guarantee either success or failure—is choosing the right people. My pastor and I spent weeks watching our people in worship and in other areas of the church. We sought out those who were actively participating in worship, but we were also looking for those people who had a passion for connecting the generations. There have been a few people who served on my teams that honestly confessed that "they couldn't carry a tune if you put it in a bucket for them." However, they were engaged in worship—they actively sought out God's revelation of himself and sought to respond in an appropriate manner. There is more to worship than just music and singing—but that is a whole different discussion! We were careful to seek out people of all ages. At the time, I was a young adult with three small children. We were really connected to that age group in our church. So, I had to move beyond my comfort zone and seek out older adults. My pastor, an older median adult, had to move beyond his preferred generation to find young adults who would be effective on the team. The selection process was long and involved, but through prayerful consideration, God placed those on the team who needed to be there.

Our first team was made up of an older child, a student, a young adult, a median adult, and a couple of senior adults. Some of the members were actively involved in the music ministry—either in choirs or handbells. Two of the members were professed non-singers, but they were adults with a keen interest in seeing the generations come together—particularly the emerging generations. Some were Bible study teachers; others were involved in student or children's ministry. The team represented a very good cross section of the church. Most importantly, they were excited about the process and eager to get started.

To avoid the dreaded creative burnout, we changed the team members periodically. You can do this in a couple of different ways: (1) Select team members for a set amount of time. For example, when you enlist team members, explain that their term will last for a season (six months, eight months, twelve months, etc.). At the conclusion of that time, reconstitute the team with new members. (2) Establish a rotating schedule for team members. Team members can be on the team for six months, then they rotate off and come back on six months later. In changing the team members often, you not only keep the team's creativity fresh, but you also engage a wider spectrum of the congregation in the ministry.

Team Operations: The Idea Session

Once the team was selected, it was time to start meeting. We determined that there would be two different types of meetings for the team: an idea session and regular sessions. The idea session happened every six to eight weeks (or about six times per year). In this meeting, the team would brainstorm creative ideas for connecting the generations in worship. We send out sermon topics and texts in advance so that the members could study and allow God to reveal himself through his word. We would have other relevant information at the ready (e.g., Lord's Supper schedule, planned special music, other planned activities that would impact our weekly worship gatherings). Armed with all the pertinent information, the team would begin to sketch out ideas for intentional integration. We would answer the following questions:

How Can I Be Intentionally Intergenerational in Worship?

- What has God revealed to me through the study of his word in the proposed sermon texts?
- How can we communicate those truths to children, to students, and to adults that will help to spiritually form them?
- How can we encourage the body to work together—across generational lines—to understand their role in worship?
- What is the big picture that we are trying to communicate? How can we communicate the big idea in a way that the youngest and oldest member of the congregation will understand and take hold of it?

The answers to these questions would provide an overarching template for specific worship elements that would encourage intentional intergenerational participation. The idea session was for painting with a broad brush, and there were several principles that were set in stone:

1. No idea was a silly/dumb idea. Many, many times, we found that the most outlandish suggestion would spark an idea that may be less "out there" but more effective.
2. Everyone had a voice. When working with an intergenerational group, many times the youngest members could be too intimidated to speak up. We specifically created a safe space where our youngest team members were encouraged when they participated. We would run with all ideas and see where they led.
3. What was discussed in CWTF stayed in CWTF. Many times we would talk about connection issues between the generations, and those issues remained private.

Once we had a good number of broad ideas for the coming season, it was time to hone in and make specific decisions related to each individual service.

Team Operations: Regular Sessions

After the idea session for a new season was concluded, the team would then begin to meet either weekly or biweekly to establish concrete plans that could be carried out in the upcoming worship services. In the regular meetings, the team would take the big idea and find elements that would communicate the idea intergenerationally. Worship elements could take the

Planning for Intergenerational Worship

form of video, drama, congregational music, special music, scenic ideas, lighting plans. We would also branch out into ways of doing the welcome, Scripture reading, or even the announcements. We sought to always answer the question, What would help all our congregational members to feel a sense of belonging?

The regular meetings would always begin with a brain-stretching exercise. We would employ brain teasers or puzzles to move out of the mundane workaday world. Then we would take a look at what had happened in worship since the last meeting. What elements were particularly effective and which activities were not effective—and why? The team would then look at the services several weeks out. My goal is to have at least the next eight weeks of services planned. In doing so, it gives both the team and the leadership time to make adjustments to better incorporate all the generations. We would use an intergenerational involvement chart to track moments of intentional intergenerational connectivity in our services (see fig. 9.1).

How Can I Be Intentionally Intergenerational in Worship?

	Last Week	This Week	Next Week	2 Weeks	3 Weeks	4 Weeks
Welcome	Addie Lynn (senior adult)	Pastor Ricky	Bobby/George (Grand Parent/Grandson)	Smith Family (3 generations)	David	Susan/Debbie (Mother/Daughter)
Call to Worship		Sarah (student) Reading Ps 95		Psalm 8 Reader's Theater	Child Reading Ps 145	Jacob (student) Reading Ps 150
Music		Children's Choir sings		Student Choir leads	Senior Adult Choir in Loft	Preschool Choir sings
Music				Student Choir leads	Senior Adult Choir	
Scripture	James (6th grader)		Brad/Stephanie (young parents)	John (3rd grader)	Brian and Judy (seniors)	Fred (senior adult)
Sermon						
Response						
Communion	Small stations around WC				Participation by families	
Sending						
Announcements	Intergen Video	Intergen Video	Intergen Video	Intergen Video	Intergen Video	Intergen Video

Figure 9.1. Intergenerational involvement chart

Using the chart above helps track how we are intentionally connecting the generations through the worship elements. The categories can change over time as elements are added to the plan.

CONCLUDING THOUGHTS

Let's return to that very first CWTF my pastor and I created so many years ago. The output of that team went far beyond what we could have ever imagined from our vocational staff perspectives. The team even moved beyond worship and began to closely examine every element of our church for its intergenerational impact. The results of those conversations led the church to complete a renovation of our worship center. They also took an old church parlor, in a prime location on our campus but very rarely used, and created an inviting welcome center and coffee bar. That welcome center became a gathering place for young and old alike. In fact, in a funny story, our second-grade son's Sunday school teacher berated us several times because our child was always late to Sunday school. He was late because he was hanging out in the welcome center, drinking coffee with some of the older men in our church. Now that is intergenerationality put into motion. While he should have been in Sunday school, he was creating intergenerational connections that helped to weave him into the fabric of our church.

While the Creative Worship Task Force can be an effective tool for creating moments of intergenerational connectivity in worship, it may not be right for every congregation. Seeking to relinquish some control over the elements of worship can be daunting to any worship leader at the very least. Each minister must decide if the benefits of team planning outweigh the downsides. Whether you use a CWTF or plan worship elements yourself, the next step is putting all those plans into play through leading intergenerational worship.

QUESTIONS FOR THOUGHT AND DISCUSSION

1. Would my congregation benefit from creating a CWTF?
2. Who are the people in my congregation who would be able to serve well in this kind of team?
3. How can I adapt the CWTF idea to best suit the needs of my congregation?

10

Leading Intergenerational Worship

AT THIS POINT IN THE BOOK, I want you to take a moment and pause for reflection. We have discussed many different concepts that all lead toward integrating the generations in worship. We have talked about intentional mutuality, or ways that we can intentionally plan for the generations to come together during worship. We've examined aspects of planning and creating a team that can help to guide the process.

Now, think back to the story of my childhood church I shared earlier in the introduction. There are children in your congregation who are "orphaned" just as I was. They may have a single parent sitting with them, or they may just be coming with friends. They may just be sitting alone while their parents are involved in leadership roles as were my siblings and me. They are in your pews. But even more than that, there are orphaned adults and particularly senior adults sitting in your pews as well. They may be survivors of a nasty divorce. They could be recently widowed. They also could have recently graduated from college and moved to your city to start a new career. Whatever their story, they are just as alone.

INTERGENERATIONAL WORSHIP IS FORMATIONAL

Are there ways to plan and lead services that can connect these orphans with others? The answer, of course, is a definite yes! We have children who need to come under the mentorship of an "adopted" grandparent almost as much as those grandparents need to show love and encouragement to them. As a new grandparent whose only grandchild is preparing to move over one thousand miles away, I can definitely understand the desire to live out those grandparental instincts and am looking for those who might need that encouragement. There are young adults who need to connect with median adults who can serve as role models for both their careers and their spiritual walks. It all boils down to this: we *need* each other.

Earlier in the book, we discussed how formational worship can be for each of us walking through the Christian life. God uses our experiences in worship to conform us into the image of Christ. Imagine, if you will, a group of children sequestered in a separate room and left to their own devices for worship—à la *The Lord of the Flies*. How long would it take until total anarchy sets in? How would they begin to understand their place and role in worship without guidance from more mature believers? Children need to see parents and grandparents, aunts and uncles, and even student role models worship. They need us. Moreover, we need them.

Now imagine a church that is devoid of children, students, and young adults. How long would it take for that church to simply become the custodian of "organ recitals" (prayer request sessions over whose kidneys were failing and who needed joint replacement surgery) and funerals? Adults need to see and experience the spark of fervor that happens when a child or a student comes to know Christ. They can be both inspirational and motivational for the rest of us who had maybe become complacent about our faith.

Tangible Ways to Lead Intentionally

With those pictures firmly planted in our minds, allow me to ask a question: What are some tangible ways that we can both intentionally plan and lead our church toward generational connections? Allow me to suggest just a few ideas right up front. First, create an "Adopt-A-Person" program. I used to say "Adopt-A-Child" but as we have already seen, there are other disconnected people attending our weekly gatherings. Start by identifying children who are "Sunday orphans"—those coming alone or whose parents are busy. Connect them with an older adult as an adopted grandparent, aunt, or uncle for the service. As the connections grow, you might see those connections blossom even outside the walls of the church as those adopted adults attend ball games or school events—further enriching the connections. Then, you also need to identify those single/unconnected adults. Pair them with an older adult, a student, or even a family. Encourage them to

How Can I Be Intentionally Intergenerational in Worship?

get involved with the others. It may be uncomfortable at first, but you will soon see benefits.

Second, include all age groups as part of your worship leadership teams. There is nothing so sweet as to see all generations expressing themselves in worship—together! For example, a few years ago we decided to break out of the box. Our church has been a multigenerational church since its inception almost seventy-five years ago. We have families with several generations participating together in Bible study and worship. We have been doing the whole "multigen worship" thing for many years. We would plan a special service, practice the music (in separate rehearsals), then come together for a final dress rehearsal before the service. Those services were always sweet times of worship, but something was missing. There was an element of connection that just was not happening. As soon as the music portion of the service ended, the children and students would make their way to their normal seats and life would resume as usual.

One year, we decided to do something much more intentional. For the summer, our children's ministry dismissed their normal Wednesday night activities and joined the adults in choir rehearsal. We had several fellowships with fun foods that would appeal sometimes to the adults and sometimes to the kids. Every week, our adults would join in and play silly games with the children. One of my favorite pictures from this summer was a sweet, retired lady competing with a child in one of our silly games. We hung donuts from the ceiling and the competitors had to eat the donut without using their hands. Being willing to get down on their level and play their games was an invaluable step in connecting the generations in our church. At the end of the summer, we worshiped together with the whole church family. Even five months later, we still had children joining us every week in the choir loft because they were connected! It wasn't just about the silly games and the fellowship—the difference was made because we were being intentional about making connections across generational lines. We may never know the full impact of those few months together, but we joyfully continue this practice to this day.

There are other ways to connect young and old in worship leadership. One of the simplest ways is to put them on your leadership teams. Yes, there is a way to do this effectively. From the very beginning, though, you must expand your concept of worship leadership teams. When we say worship leadership teams, we automatically think of worship leaders, praise teams, or even praise bands. However, I hope that you will realize that there are so many others who help lead in worship week by week. Think about this: what is the first thing that happens when the lyrics appear out of order during a worship song? The people lose focus in worship. What happens when a microphone doesn't get turned on in time or is not muted fast enough? The people lose focus in worship. In other words, those who serve on your media teams are worship leaders just as much as those who stand behind the microphones.

When you are selecting members for your media teams, do not forget that there is a whole generation of people who have never known life without technology. Your older children and students can be incredible assets to your media teams. Allow me to share a story with you. It was many years ago, and we were serving in a church way out in West Texas. The staff decided to incorporate projection screens as a part of our worship services. We were very methodical with how we introduced them. We started slowly, just using it for projecting the notes for the sermon. We then expanded to placing the hymn titles and numbers on the screen. Finally, we introduced the lyrics. At this point, I needed some help. I turned to one of our "techy" students and taught him how to run PowerPoint. He treasured being asked to help and became my most faithful media volunteer. I eventually taught him how to run audio and lighting as well. He was mentored both by me as the minister of music and by the other adults on the team. Why am I telling you this story? Yes, it was a sweet time of generational connection. But more than that—fast forward fifteen years in the future and I hired that same kid as a full-time media minister for the church in which I was serving. He is still serving his church through the media ministry to this day. You will never fully understand the impact that generational connections can have.

Think about those who are serving with your greeting and usher teams every week. I still remember my high school days when the high school boys were the people designated to take up the offering on Sunday nights. We felt like we were the "big dogs!" We followed the lead of those adults who did the same thing on Sunday mornings—and we had a role to play in worship leadership. Your greeting teams are also a great place for intergenerational service. Using children, students, young adults, and older adults on these teams both connects them to serving the church and gives them a role to play in how we worship. An additional byproduct is that when we use people of all ages on our welcome teams, all ages begin to feel that sense of belongingness.

How Can I Be Intentionally Intergenerational in Worship?

There are other places where an older child or student might be able to serve in worship leadership. I've already told you the story about our choir this summer. We still have children joining the choir every Sunday morning because of the connections that were made this summer. They are learning that they can have a place and a role in worship leadership. More than that, you may have students who are participating in their school band or orchestra programs. Think about how many true generational connections can be made when you invite a student to come and play with your orchestra/band. They sit beside adults who have had a lifetime of experiences in living the Christian life. They might not always be the most gifted players, but you will be amazed by how much improvement you see as the adults take them under their wings and mentor them.

Include people of all ages in various worship elements during your worship service. In the last chapter, I shared the intergenerational involvement chart with you. Use the chart as a tool to make sure that you are including people of every generation in every service. One of the most effective things we have done is to use people of varying ages to read Scripture each week. In chapter 11, you will find many ways to employ every generation in the reading of Scripture through responsorial readings, storytelling, reader's theaters, and other methods. The most important concept to consider is that you be intentional. Just asking a child to read a Scripture every once in a while is not being intentional. Plan how you will use them effectively and methodically.

You could also add a student or older child to your praise team rotation. Much like young people playing in your orchestra, those who come alongside your singers will grow both in their faith and in their musicianship. Is it always perfect? No, but I can think of no better way to encourage connections across generational lines than to have children and students serving with the adults on the platform week after week. Remember when we talked about creating a sense of belongingness? How much more connected would our children and students feel if they walked in and saw people just like them serving in places of leadership all over the worship center?

Breaking the Status Quo

There are other issues you may need to consider as you intentionally plan for generational connectedness. As you seek to add young adults to your leadership teams, you may need to think about their life-stage situations. Many of them will not feel able to serve because they have young children with whom they need to sit. What can you adjust to help them connect and participate? You could set up a rotation schedule so that they are only serving once per month. You could help to find "adopted" adults to sit with their children while they serve. You may need to adjust the way you lead your ministries. Think about allowing your choir and other musical leadership to exit the platform when the music portion of the service concludes.

There may be well-established patterns in your church that may need to be broken or adjusted to create opportunities for intergenerational interaction. Consider where people sit in worship. We are all creatures of habit, and we like to sit in the same place, surrounded by the same people each week. Your students may sit all together at the back, in the balcony, or even in the front of the worship center. Think about ways to encourage people to move around. I was very fortunate to have a pastor who allowed me eight Sunday nights to teach a worship study to our people. As a part of that study, I encouraged them to "sit different." In other words, I encouraged them to move around the worship center each Sunday. Not only did several long-time members do so, but I was astonished at how many of them told me how many new people they got to know and how much they enjoyed the process. Consider bringing your student pastor on board and creating a new paradigm for seating in the worship center. Brainstorm ideas with them that will encourage your students to spread out and meet the older adults. You may be surprised by the effect.

Whatever you do, do it intentionally. Plan the process and work the plan. We all know the story of how to boil a frog. If you take a frog and throw it into a pot of boiling water, the frog will simply jump out. However, if you place the frog in a pot of cool water and slowly and methodically bring up the temperature, the frog will sit there until he becomes someone's dinner. Be methodical. Be wise. Be intentional.

In the following chapter, you will find many intentional tools that can be used in worship for fostering intergenerational connections. I hope that you will read through them and let them spark your own creativity. The tools and ideas listed are not an exhaustive list, they are merely a starting point. Every church cultus is different. Build on the ideas listed to formulate activities and ministry service that "fits" your church.

11

Resources for Being Intentionally Intergenerational in Worship

ONE OF THE MOST difficult challenges worship planners and leaders face today is creating elements of worship that are intentionally focused on engaging all the generations in worship. From the moment the doors to the worship center open to the closing benediction, leaders must consistently give attention to intentionally encouraging the interaction of all congregants. Whether through participation in reading and singing, or simply listening and watching something happening on the platform, we are charged with the task of promoting intergenerational interaction in all aspects of the worship service.

In the following pages, I have sought to find ways to encourage intergenerational interaction in many of the elements of worship we use every week. This list is by no means exhaustive. On the contrary, it is my hope that you will use the following ideas as a springboard for creating worship elements that will truly engage your congregants in intergenerational relationships that could spark a revival of truly intergenerational worship times.

BEFORE THE DOORS OPEN

- Have a plan in place that will utilize people of all generations.
  - Use fathers and sons to direct people from the parking lot to the entrance.

- If your church uses a shuttle system (e.g., golf carts), consider using parent/child teams to facilitate. The parent can drive, and the child/student can welcome people and help those who might need a little assistance.
- Incorporate a low frequency FM radio transmitter to help welcome people onto your church campus.
  - Have signs telling folks the frequency to which they need to tune.
  - Incorporate families of all ages (young parents with children, empty nesters, and senior adults) in the recordings used to welcome people to church and help prepare them for the Bible study, fellowship, and worship that will occur during their visit.
  - The recording loop can also alert guests about where they can park and which doors to enter.
- Use families to welcome people to church.
  - Parents and older children can open doors for those coming inside.
  - Our church provides small signs for younger children to hold. The signs utilize welcome messages that rotate throughout the year. The younger children in our church get so excited holding up those signs.

CALLING/WELCOMING GOD'S PEOPLE TO WORSHIP

- Use family groups (i.e., father/sons, mother/daughters, grandparents/grandchildren) to welcome congregants at the doors as they arrive for worship.
  - Adults can shake hands and offer a word of welcome.
  - Children can hand out the weekly worship bulletin.
  - Not only does using family groups help to create a sense of belonging for various generations, but it also helps to instill an understanding of the importance of serving others in the children.
- Invite multiple generations to offer a spoken welcome to worship at the beginning of the service.

How Can I Be Intentionally Intergenerational in Worship?

- Use a family group to welcome the congregation.
- Use intergenerational groupings to offer a simultaneous welcome across the congregation.
  - At a prearranged signal, groups of two or three people from different generations stand and welcome small sections of people in the worship center at the same time.
  - The leaders offer words of welcome and then lead their section in a short time of prayer asking God to prepare them for worship.
  - Depending on the size of the worship space, there could be dozens of small welcome times happening at once.
  - The intimacy of the greeting assists in creating a sense of belongingness and encourages participation in the service to follow.

READING SCRIPTURE IN WORSHIP

- Use readers of various ages.
- Creatively use technology to incorporate readers of varying generations in reading Scripture.
  - With the advent of the COVID-19 pandemic, many churches were forced into utilizing video for their services. Instead of approaching the task begrudgingly, consider how we might employ that technology to intentionally include others in worship leadership.
  - Use multiple ages to read a single passage of Scripture. In the editing room, cut together single words or small phrases from the various readers to form a complete reading.
  - Use video to include those who might not be able to normally attend (e.g., nursing home/assisted living residents, deployed members of the military, etc.).
- Creatively employ responsive readings and responsorial readings[234]

---

234. There is a slight difference between responsive and responsorial readings. A responsive reading usually incorporates the recitation of Scripture in an alternating fashion. A leader will begin and the congregation will follow with the next phrase or verse. On the other hand, a responsorial reading is commonly a Scripture or other reading with a repeated refrain. In this instance, the leader will read Scripture and the congregation

◦ Many denominational hymnals include topical responsive readings. Other readings for the day may be adapted to be read responsively, giving the congregation an opportunity to speak the words of Scripture.

Psalm 100

(A Responsive Reading)

Leader
Make a joyful noise to the Lord, all the earth!

Congregation
Serve the Lord with gladness!
Come into his presence with singing!

Leader
Know that the Lord, he is God!
It is he who made us, and we are his;

Congregation
We are his people, and the sheep of his pasture.

Leader
Enter his gates with thanksgiving
And his courts with praise!

Congregation
Give thanks to him; bless his name!

Leader
For the Lord is good;
His steadfast love endures forever,

Congregation
And his faithfulness to all generations.

---

will respond with a repeated phrase (see Psalm 136).

How Can I Be Intentionally Intergenerational in Worship?

Philippians 2:5–11

(A Responsive Reading)

Leader
Have this mind among yourselves,
which is yours in Christ Jesus,
Who, though he was in the form of God,
did not count equality with God a thing to be grasped,

Congregation
But emptied himself, by taking the form of a servant,
being born in the likeness of men.

Leader
And being found in human form,
he humbled himself by becoming obedient to the point of death,
even death on a cross.

Congregation
Therefore God has highly exalted him
and bestowed on him the name that is above every name.

Leader
So that at the name of Jesus every knee should bow,
in heaven and on earth and under the earth,

Congregation
And every tongue confess that Jesus Christ is Lord,
to the glory of God the Father.

- Responsorial Readings: Psalm 136 includes a repeated refrain following each verse that is easily learned and repeated by all congregational members.

Resources for Being Intentionally Intergenerational in Worship

Psalm 136

(Responsorial Psalm from Scripture)

Leader
Give thanks to the Lord, for he is good
Congregation
for his steadfast love endures forever.
Leader
Give thanks to the God of gods
Congregation
for his steadfast love endures forever.
Leader
Give thanks to the Lord of lords,
Congregation
for his steadfast love endures forever (and so on).

- Create new responsorial readings or adapted responsorial readings.

Psalm 100

(New Adaptation of a Responsorial Psalm)

Leader
Make a joyful noise to the Lord, all the earth!
Congregation
Praise ye the Lord!

Leader
Serve the Lord with gladness!
Come into his presence with singing!
Congregation
Praise ye the Lord!

Leader
Know that the Lord, he is God!
It is he who made us, and we are his;
we are his people, and the sheep of his pasture.

How Can I Be Intentionally Intergenerational in Worship?

Congregation
Praise ye the Lord!

Leader
Enter his gates with thanksgiving,
and his courts with praise!
Give thanks to him; bless his name!
Congregation
Praise ye the Lord!

Leader
For the Lord is good;
his steadfast love endures forever,
and his faithfulness to all generations.
Congregation
Praise ye the Lord!

Psalm 146

(New Adaptation of a Responsorial Psalm)

Leader
Praise the Lord!
Praise the Lord, O my soul!
Congregation
I will praise the Lord as long as I live;
I will sing praises to my God while I have my being.

Leader
Put not your trust in princes,
In a son of man, in whom there is no salvation
Congregation
I will praise the Lord as long as I live;
I will sing praises to my God while I have my being.

Leader
When his breath departs, he returns to the earth;
On that very day his plans perish.

Congregation
I will praise the Lord as long as I live;
I will sing praises to my God while I have my being.

Leader
Blessed is he whose help is the God of Jacob,
Whose hope is in the Lord his god.
Congregation
I will praise the Lord as long as I live;
I will sing praises to my God while I have my being.

Psalm 118

(New Psalm Adaptation for Child-led Responsorial Reading)

Child Leader
Give thanks to the Lord, for he is good!
Congregation
His faithful love lasts forever.

Child Leader
Let all of the people repeat,
Congregation
His faithful love lasts forever.

Child Leader
Let everyone who loves the Lord repeat,
Congregation
His faithful love lasts forever.

Child Leader
This is the day the Lord has made
All
We will rejoice and be glad in it!

- Create a Scripture reading that incorporates storytelling. Storytelling allows people to give testimony to the way God has worked in their lives. Storytelling can be added to many aspects of the service. One effective way of utilizing storytelling is to incorporate it in the reading of Scripture. Use families or individuals to illuminate certain biblical passages with anecdotal illustrations from their lives. Using Ps 136 as an example:

Psalm 136

(Paraphrase with Storytelling)

Leader (v. 1)
Give thanks to the Lord, for he is good.

Family 1
Here a family shares a testimony of no more than one minute of a time when they have experienced God's goodness.

Congregation
For his steadfast love endures forever.

Leader (v. 16)
To him who led his people through the wilderness.

Family 2
Here a family shares a testimony of no more than one minute of a time when God brought them through a difficult situation.

Congregation
For his steadfast love endures forever.

Leader (vv. 23–24)
It is he who remembered us in our low estate, and rescued us from our foes.

Family 3
Here a family shares a testimony of no more than one minute of a time when God rescued their family from a crisis.

Congregation

Resources for Being Intentionally Intergenerational in Worship

For his steadfast love endures forever.

- Use family groups as readers.
- Read Scripture aloud together. Many times, leaders simply read Scripture over our congregations. Allow them to participate through reading together.
- Encourage parents and other adults to involve young pre-readers by allowing them to follow along as the adult points to the words in their copy of the Scripture.
- Create and rehearse "Reader's Theatre" Scripture readings involving multiple generations. Reader's Theaters are adaptations of Scripture using the text as a basis and adding additional elements that help to reinforce the themes of the text.

Psalm 8

A Reader's Theater

by David Tatum

Student	Lord, our Lord, How majestic is your name in all the earth!
Child 1	He is magnificent!
Child 2	He is amazing!
Child 1	He is God!
Adult	Through the praise of children you have established a stronghold against your enemies, to silence the foe and the avenger.
Child 2	God is my strong tower.
Child 1	God is my fortress.
Child 2	God is my strength.
Student	When I consider your heavens, the work of your fingers,
Child 1	the moon
Child 2	and the stars
Child 1	that you have put into the sky,

Adult	What is man that you are mindful of him, the son of man that you care for him?
Child 2	You have made him a little lower than the angels.
Child 1	You have crowned him with glory and honor.
Child 2	You made him to rule over all creation.
Child 1	You put everything under his control:
Student	All the flocks and herds,
Child 2	All the animals in the fields,
Child 1	All the birds flying in the air,
Child 2	All the fish that swim in the sea.
Adult	O Lord, our Lord,
All	How majestic is your name in all the earth!

2 Peter 1:3–8

A Reader's Theater

(Before singing *Standing On the Promises*)

by David Tatum

Sr. Adult	By his divine power, God has given us everything we need for living a godly life. We have received all of this by coming to know him, the one who called us to himself by means of his marvelous glory and excellence.
Adult	And because of his glory and excellence, he has given us great and precious promises. These are the promises that enable you to share his divine nature and escape the world's corruption caused by human desires.

Resources for Being Intentionally Intergenerational in Worship

Student	In view of all this, make every effort to respond to God's promises.
Child 1	Add to your faith, goodness;
Child 2	and to goodness, knowledge;
Child 1	and to knowledge, self-control;
Child 2	and to self-control, patient endurance;
Child 1	and to patient endurance, godliness;
Child 2	and to godliness, brotherly affection;
Child 1	and to brotherly affection, love for everyone.
Student	The more you grow like this, the more productive and useful you will be in your knowledge of our Lord Jesus Christ.

Isaiah 40:28–31

A Reader's Theater

by David Tatum

Child 1	Do you not know?
Child 2	Have you not heard?
Student	The LORD is the everlasting God, the Creator of the whole earth.
Adult	He never becomes faint or weary;
Child 1	God doesn't get tired!
Child 2	He *never* needs a nap!
Student	There is no limit to his understanding.
Child 2	God knows everything!

How Can I Be Intentionally Intergenerational in Worship?

Child 1	He even understands my math homework!
Adult	He gives strength to the faint and strengthens the powerless.
Child 1	When I don't think I can do it...
Child 2	God will give me strength to finish!
Student	Young people may become faint and weary, and young men stumble and fall,
Adult	But those who trust in the Lord will renew their strength; they will soar on wings like eagles.
Child 2	Can you imagine flying like an eagle?
Child 1	Yeah, spreading my wings and soaring so high you couldn't even see me.
All	We shall run and not be weary; we shall walk and not faint.

Praying in Worship

- Use various age groups to lead times of prayer.
- Use written prayers.
  - Spoken by multigenerational leaders.
  - Read in unison by the congregation.
- Use historic prayers as a part of the service.
  - Resource: *The Valley of Vision: A Collection of Puritan Prayers and Devotions.*

Resources for Being Intentionally Intergenerational in Worship

MEETING GOD[235]

(HISTORIC PRAYERS OF GOD'S PEOPLE)

GREAT GOD,
    In public and private, in sanctuary and home,
        may my life be steeped in prayer,
        filled with the spirit of grace and supplication,
        each prayer perfumed with the incense of atoning blood.
    Help me, defend me, until from praying ground
        I pass to the realm of unceasing praise.
    Urged by my need, invited by thy promises, called by thy Spirit,
        I enter thy presence, worshiping thee with godly fear,
            awed by thy majesty, greatness, glory,
            but encouraged by thy love.
I am all poverty as well as all guilt,
        having nothing of my own with which to repay thee,
But I bring Jesus to thee in arms of faith,
        pleading his righteousness to offset my iniquities,
        rejoicing that he will weigh down the scales for me,
            and satisfy thy justice.
I bless thee that great sin draws out great grace,
        that, although the least sin deserves infinite punishment
        because done against an infinite God,
            yet there is mercy for me,
            for where guilt is most terrible,
            there thy mercy in Christ is most free and deep.
Bless me by revealing to me more of his saving merits,
        by causing thy goodness to pass before me,
        by speaking peace to my contrite heart;
Strengthen me to give thee no rest
        until Christ shall reign supreme within me,
        in every thought, word, and deed,
        in a faith that purifies the heart,
            overcomes the world, works by love,
            fastens me to thee,
            and ever clings to the cross.

---

235. Bennett, *Valley of Vision*, 148.

How Can I Be Intentionally Intergenerational in Worship?

- Create times for a "Concert of Prayer."
    - All members of the congregation pray together simultaneously.
    - Congregants all pray aloud.
- Utilize family pairs to pray (e.g., father/son, mother/daughter, grandparent/grandchild).
- Divide the congregation into family groups for a directed prayer time. Encourage families to "adopt" those who do not have family present.

SINGING IN WORSHIP

- Choose music from a variety of musical styles.
    - Understand your church's musical culture and rely on music that supports that culture.
    - Stretch the people of every generation with styles that fall outside their normal comfort zones.
    - Choose music that is theologically sound.
        > Worship leaders must be very careful to guard the words they place in the mouths of their parishioners. Holly Allen contends that "we need to sing songs that will take up residence in their hearts for their entire lives."[236]
        > Most people do not walk away from a worship service recounting the points of the sermon. However, they will walk away humming or even singing the songs that were a part of the worship time.
    - Choose music that is singable by the congregation.
        > Choose or transpose songs into singable keys. Most popular worship songs and many older hymns are pitched too high for most singers.
        > Choose music that is melodically interesting but rhythmically attainable.

---

236. Allen, "Best Practices for Worship."

Resources for Being Intentionally Intergenerational in Worship

- * Simplify double-dotted, syncopated rhythms of many popular songs.
- * Simplify melodic lines of popular songs.
- ▫ Choose music that can be understood on some level by members of every generation or include teaching times in the service that will aid in comprehension and appreciation. Knowing the background story of the writing of a particular song helps to give contextual meaning.

- After choosing appropriate music for the service, plan ways to intentionally involve members of all generations. Remember that a sense of belonging is more easily attained when the platform personnel are a generational and ethnic cross section of the church body.
  - ▫ Utilize all age groups in vocal leadership positions.
    - ▸ Use older elementary, middle school, and high school students as well as young, median, and senior adults on leadership teams.
    - ▸ Create an intergenerational choir.
  - ▫ Utilize all age groups in instrumental leadership positions.
    - ▸ Incorporate young players in instrumental groups.
    - ▸ Musical mentoring relationships can happen when you intentionally seat a young musician with an older, experienced musician.

- Consider creating a season focused on intergenerational worship. This past summer, the church I serve as worship leader decided to focus on intentional intergenerational connections in the music ministry. We planned for an end-of-summer musical service that would be led by intergenerational teams. However, instead of practicing in separate rehearsals, our children's minister bought in and gave up most of their Wednesday evening activities for the summer—only retaining a few special events on these regularly scheduled service nights. Instead, our adult choir, some students, and all our children all met together each week for rehearsal and fellowship. The adults played silly games with the children, and the young people were mentored through rehearsals by adults. I cannot express how sweet that time became for all of us. New connections between adult worship leaders and our students and

How Can I Be Intentionally Intergenerational in Worship?

children were forged and will help us maintain those relationships as we move back to age-segregated meetings during the school year.

Media in Worship

- Utilize all age groups in media and technical leadership groups.
  - Use all age groups from children to senior adults in behind-the-scenes roles like media ministry.
  - Create an audio/visual ministry apprenticeship where older children and students come alongside experienced adults in learning the various aspects of the media ministry (e.g., audio, camera operations, lighting, projected media, broadcast/streaming media, etc.).
  - Create a video team that produces video segments for use in services (e.g., video announcements, theme interpretation, testimonies, etc.).
    - Use every generation as "on-screen talent." Feature all the generations in video segments. For example, include a child or student as a part of the video announcements.
    - Utilize the technical skills of young people in the editing and production of videos. Do not forget to celebrate the intergenerational media team for their contributions to worship leadership.
- Utilize all age groups in a Creative Worship Task Force (see chapter 9).

Speaking to God's People in Worship (Other Spoken Words)

- Use transition times between worship elements to engage members of all generations.
- The Children's Sermon:
  - If used, direct the content to the children and not the congregation.

Resources for Being Intentionally Intergenerational in Worship

- Ensure that it is integrally woven into the thematic fabric and structure of the service.
- Provide the children an avenue of active response.
  - Invite them to memorize a portion of Scripture from the sermon.
  - Encourage them to listen for special words or phrases in the remainder of the service.

- Encourage the use of testimonies in worship.
  - Incorporate baptism videos as a part of your services. These videos will introduce the new believers in your church family and will give them an opportunity to speak into the lives of all the members of your church.
  - Incorporate random testimonies as a regular part of your service. Utilize members of all age groups to share testimonies regarding big events, mission trips, life issues and struggles, evangelistic attempts, or moments when God's hand was truly seen to be at work.
  - Here are some ideas to consider when planning testimonies:
    - Consider using video for testimonies. The video format allows the worship planner to control the time and content of the testimony. Some of the scariest moments I have had in worship leadership have been when I placed a mic in the hands of someone for a testimony time.
    - Give parameters to those preparing to share a testimony:
      * Time limit
      * Theme
      * Is there anything you particularly want them to emphasize? For example, if they are sharing about a mission trip experience, what aspect of the trip do you want them to speak about? What are some topics you want them to avoid?
    - Consider rehearsing the testimonies in the place where they will be given. A rehearsal will give you an opportunity to hear and redirect the content but will also give them confidence in knowing the logistical aspects of their testimony.

How Can I Be Intentionally Intergenerational in Worship?

Confessing Our Sin in Worship

- Read confessional Scripture.
  - Using ideas and patterns discussed above in reading Scripture, have the congregation read confessional passages.
    - Ps 51, Isa 6, etc.
- Pray confessional prayers.
  - Pray silently and individually.
  - Use members of different generations to pray a prayer of corporate confession.
- Allow space and time for response.
  - Distribute small pieces of paper to everyone in the congregation.
  - Allow time for contemplation, reflection, and prayers of individual confession.
  - Have congregants write their confessed sins on the pieces of paper.
  - Congregants may then come to the front and use a small hammer to nail their sins to a cross constructed for this service.
  - In another special service, we have used the same process listed above but instead of nailing it to a cross, we went outside and placed the slips of paper in a large vessel and burned them. In this method, there is some additional symbolism. The sins are gone, but the consequences from those sins (ashes) still remain.
  - You could also use magician's flash paper for this process. Flash paper looks like regular paper, but when set alight, completely disappears in a flash of flame.

Gathering Around God's Table in Worship (Communion)

- Use the Lord's Supper for adding physical movement to the service.
  - The physicality of standing and moving from one place to another helps to reengage the mind of all generations.

Resources for Being Intentionally Intergenerational in Worship

- Move to designated areas to receive the elements.
- As a result of the COVID-19 pandemic, my church has adjusted the way we traditionally participate in the Lord's Supper. Instead of sitting quietly and waiting for the elements to be passed, our congregation now moves to the front and receives the elements.
- For special observances, have the people move to smaller stations situated around the worship center. The stations can be decorated to further engage the senses.
- Using an automatic bread machine to bake bread during the service can also help to further engage the senses.

- Young children and the Lord's Supper:
  - Robbie Castleman suggests that for young children, "anticipation is the best preparation."[237]
  - Castleman relates that when her children were too young to participate, she would hold the elements in her hands and have the children cup their hands around hers. While doing so, she would explain the significance of the moment to them in a whisper.[238]
  - Catherine Stonehouse and Scottie May suggest that children move forward with other participants, but instead of receiving the elements, they receive a blessing from the communicant, thereby helping them to feel a part of the celebration.[239]
  - David Csinos and Ivy Beckwith advocate for children to participate in the Lord's Supper through guided practice.[240] In guided practice, young children are led through the steps and taught the symbolism and meaning behind the memorial meal by a parent or other mentor.

- Participate by family groups.
  - Much like the celebration of the Passover in the Old Testament, encourage fathers to lead their families in participation.

---

237. Castleman, *Parenting in the Pew*, 126.
238. Castleman, *Parenting in the Pew*, 126–127.
239. Stonehouse and May, *Listening to Children*, 69.
240. Csinos and Beckwith, *Children's Ministry*, 121.

How Can I Be Intentionally Intergenerational in Worship?

- As fathers lead, they can bring younger, nonparticipating children into the story and symbolism of the supper.
- Allow ample time in the service for fathers to explain the celebration and lead their families to participate.
- Create a written guide for fathers outlining the steps, Scriptures, and meaning/symbolism behind each element of the Supper.
- Encourage families to "adopt" singles and others who do not have families present to become part of their family for the day.
- Encourage young families to "adopt" senior adults as special grandparents for the celebration.

• Create times for a come-and-go, family-based Communion Celebration.

- Open the church for times where families can come and celebrate the Lord's Supper outside the normal services of the church. One church we served opened the church for a come-and-go Lord's Supper on Christmas Eve. The time was not minister-led, but rather overseen by our deacon body and family led. We provided written materials as described above to allow fathers to lead their families.
- Other possible times for a come-and-go, family-based Lord's Supper:
  - Christmas Eve
  - Maundy Thursday
  - Good Friday
  - Designated services that will be dedicated to the event (e.g., a Sunday or Wednesday night service time).

GIVING TO GOD IN WORSHIP

• Use movement so that all may be involved.
- Invite the congregation to bring their offerings to the front.
- Invite the congregation to stand.

Resources for Being Intentionally Intergenerational in Worship

- Use children, students, and adults as ushers.
- Encourage fathers to lead their families in times of giving. If necessary, create written materials to guide fathers through the process. As with other times in the service, fathers leading their families can be times of intense discipleship.
- With the surge in online giving following the COVID-19 pandemic, encourage those who have given online to participate physically in the offering by placing an empty envelope in the plate or other offering receptacle.

Physicality in Worship

- Allow for physical movement in the church.
  - Create times at intervals where the congregation can move.
    - Coming forward to celebrate the Lord's Supper.
    - Moving to bring the offering.
    - Moving during a time of confession (see suggested activity above).
  - Utilize times of sitting and standing during the worship service.
    - Sitting for extended periods of time can enable minds to wander.
    - On the other hand, standing for extended periods of time can cause weariness, especially in older participants.
- If it is part of your church culture, encourage active, physical responses in worship.
  - Clapping hands in time with the music.
  - Raising hands in worship.
  - Standing or kneeling when appropriate.

How Can I Be Intentionally Intergenerational in Worship?

Sending God's People Out to Live Lives of Worship

- Consider the question, "What does life look like for different generations (going to school, going to work, retired persons)?"
- Craft a commissioning statement that encompasses the whole of the congregation. For example:
  - "As you leave this place and enter your mission field, be it in the hallways and classrooms of your school, the cubicle of your office, or as you spend time with grandchildren or even great-grandchildren, you are the light of Christ. You are the beacon on the hill for those wandering in the darkness."
  - "God has called and commanded you to share his light with those around you who are walking in darkness. As you see friends or coworkers or family this week, let your light so shine that they will be drawn to Christ."
  - "God has gifted you with the ability to shine his light in a dark world. As you move through the hallways of your schools, as you labor alongside lost coworkers, as you walk the streets of your neighborhoods, let that light shine so that others may be drawn not to you, but to the Christ who is in you."

The Written Word

- Use bulletins and other materials to reinforce the main concepts of the service.
  - Include space for note taking during the sermon.
    - Include relevant spoken portions of the service.
- When we think about written words, we must also think about the media that we project each week. Here are some ideas to consider regarding intergenerational involvement:
  - Song lyrics.

Resources for Being Intentionally Intergenerational in Worship

- Use sentence case instead of all uppercase text. Uppercase text can be difficult for young readers to read.
- Pick fonts that are easily read. Try to avoid fonts that use heavy serifs, and particularly avoid script fonts as today's young readers are generally not taught to read cursive.
- Use a font size that is easily read from all areas of your congregation.
- Limit the number of words on the screens at any given time. A good rule of thumb is two lines of text per slide.

▫ Background media
- Choose background media for your presentations that will engage and not distract. Motion graphics with intense movement and/or highly contrasting color schemes may cause participants of every generation to become distracted.
- Consider coordinating color schemes for a seamless and less distracting presentation. Incorporate lighting that compliments your presentations and try to avoid drastic changes in color within a single service.
- Add media that compliments the current worship element. Our pastor seeks to use pictures as well as text during the course of his sermons. He will use text to delineate his points, and then move quickly to graphics that illustrate the point he is seeking to make. His use of graphics helps to keep the people engaged.

▫ Think intergenerationally when creating media for your services.
- Always consider the preferences of both the younger and older members of your congregation as you plan and implement projected media.
- Include items that will draw the attention of your youngest members but will still engage the oldest members of your congregation.

- Create a handout for children designed specifically for the service that week.

How Can I Be Intentionally Intergenerational in Worship?

- Include space for taking notes from the pastor's sermon. Give the children blanks to fill in as they listen.
- Include space for them to respond to what they've experienced in other aspects of the service: music, Scripture reading, prayer, welcome, etc.
- Include activities that directly relate to the thematic fabric and structure of the service. For example, if the music and sermon are focusing on the Lordship of Christ, provide a coloring picture or word activities that reinforce that concept.
- Institute a reward system for children who complete certain portions of the handout. In our church, if children complete the notes section, they can find the pastor at the end of the service, and he will give them a small piece of candy or other small reward.
- The children's handout should encourage active listening and participation throughout the entirety of the service.

ONCE THE DOORS CLOSE

- Use families to greet people as they go.
- Have older adults in the preschool to assist with child pick-up. Use adults who are gifted at making connections with young parents.
- Use intergenerational teams to do follow-up announcement videos, reminding congregants of important events during the week. Disperse the videos through the church's social media and email platforms.
- Work with the children's ministry staff to create weekday meeting times where "adopted" grandmothers can mentor young mothers.
- Create weekend events that foster intergenerational connections among the male members of your congregation. Set up a day where all the men, male students, and boys meet for fishing, hunting, or go to a sporting event.
- All of these ideas, while not directly related to worship, will increase the connectedness between the generations and allow for more opportunities of true intergenerational worship.

Appendix
The Creative Worship Task Force
The Creative Worship Task Force Job Description

OBJECTIVE

The Creative Worship Task Force exists to enhance, plan, coordinate, evaluate, and encourage the body's time of corporate worship with special attention given to intergenerational involvement.

PROCEDURES

1. Membership

- The Creative Worship Task Force will be selected by the pastor and minister of music/worship.
- The Creative Worship Task Force will include the following:
  - Pastor (as needed)
  - Minister of music/worship
  - Two to five general members (at the leadership's discretion)
- Membership is for a set period of time (usually six months to two years). After the time period, either a new team is formed or members can rotate off and be replaced by new members.

2. Creative sessions

- Idea meeting

Appendix

- The idea meeting will occur approximately every eight weeks—or six times per year—or relative to sermon series preparation.
- During the idea meeting, participants will brainstorm ideas for a set of services, sermon series, or other sequence of elements.
  - Video
  - Drama
  - Theme music
  - Songs/specials
  - Scenic ideas
  - Other creative ideas for enhancing the services
- The team will have sermon topics and Scriptures in hand as far in advance as possible, enabling each team member to pray, study, research, and prepare ideas for the idea meeting.
- The idea meeting will not focus on specific services, but rather general ideas, themes, and processes.
- The idea meeting will focus on long-range planning for worship and intergenerational connectivity.

- Regular meetings
  - The regular meetings will occur weekly or biweekly.
  - The regular meetings will involve all participants who have an active role within the next two services (this week and next week).
  - During the regular meeting, specific plans will be made for the service next week. And we will tweak the current week's service. We will evaluate the past week's service as well.
  - A general outline will be discussed for the service two weeks away.

The regular meeting will focus on short-term goals and plans in worship and growth in worship.

Appendix

Meeting Agenda
January 23rd

OBJECTIVE

The Creative Worship Task Force exists to enhance, plan, coordinate, evaluate, and encourage the body's time of corporate worship with special attention given to intergenerational involvement.

NOTES FROM JANUARY 16TH

- Build up to new service structure (2/10)
    - Pull the obvious out
    - Small changes to service structure
- Create synergy
    - Signs up the hill (à la Burma Shave)
- Intergenerational involvement
    - How were the various generations involved last week?

THIS WEEK...

- Thinking outside the box:

            mce
            mce
            mce

    Can you solve the puzzle? (Answer at the bottom of the next page)

Appendix

Answer: Three Blind Mice (they have no *i*'s!)

- Looking at *this* week
  - Are any adjustments necessary?
  - Prayer for this week
- Looking at *next* week
  - Are any adjustments necessary?
- Creative worship plans for eight weeks out
  Examining the Scripture: Psalm 78
- Creative worship plans for seven weeks out
  Examining the Scripture:
- Creative worship plans for six weeks out
  Examining the Scripture:
- Creative worship plans for five weeks out
  Examining the Scripture:
- Creative worship plans for four weeks out
  Examining the Scripture:
- Creative worship plans for three weeks out
  Examining the Scripture:

IDEAS TO CREATE SYNERGY

Bibliography

Allcock, Mary DeLaine, and Madeline Bridges. *How to Lead Children Choirs*. Nashville: Convention, 1991.

Allen, Holly Catterton. "Best Practices for Worship with All Generations." Lecture presented at the Intergenerational Worship Summit at the University of Mary Hardin-Baylor, Belton, TX, January 24, 2020.

———. "Bringing Intergenerational Worship to Your People." Lecture presented at the Intergenerational Worship Summit at the University of Mary Hardin-Baylor, Belton, TX, January 24, 2020.

———, ed. *InterGenerate: Transforming Churches Through Intergenerational Ministry*. Abilene, TX: Abilene Christian University Press, 2018.

———. "What Is Intergenerational Worship?" Lecture presented at the Intergenerational Worship Summit at the University of Mary Hardin-Baylor, Belton, TX, January 23, 2020.

Allen, Holly Catterton, and Christine Lawton Ross. "The Benefits of Intergenerality." *Journal of Discipleship & Family Ministry* 3 (2013) 16–23.

———. *Intergenerational Christian Formation: Bringing the Whole Church Together in Ministry, Community, and Worship*. Downers Grove, IL: IVP Academic, 2012.

Aniol, Scott. "Catholic Christianity." Unpublished class notes for MUMIN-7493, Southwestern Baptist Theological Seminary, Fort Worth, TX, spring 2020.

———. "Introduction." Unpublished class notes for MUMIN-7493, Southwestern Baptist Theological Seminary, Fort Worth, TX, spring 2020.

———. *Let the Little Children Come: Family Worship on Sunday (And the Other Six Days Too)*. Conway, AR: Free Grace, 2021.

Anthony, Michael, and Michelle Anthony. *A Theology for Family Ministries*. Nashville: B&H Academic, 2011.

Armstrong, Lance. *Children in Worship: The Road to Faith*. Melbourne, Australia: Joint Board of Christian Education, 1988.

Baucham, Voddie, Jr. *Family Driven Faith: Doing What It Takes to Raise Sons and Daughters Who Walk with God*. Wheaton: Crossway, 2007.

———. *Family Shepherds: Calling and Equipping Men to Lead Their Homes*. Wheaton: Crossway, 2011.

Beale, Gregory K. "Eden, the Temple, and the Church's Mission in the New Creation." *Journal of the Evangelical Theological Society* 48 (2005) 5–31.

Beeke, Joel R. *Family Worship*. Grand Rapids: Reformation Heritage, 2009.

Bibliography

Bennett, Arthur, ed. *The Valley of Vision: A Collection of Puritan Prayers and Devotions.* Carlisle, PA: Banner of Truth Trust, 1975.

Breneman, Mervin. *Ezra, Nehemiah, Esther.* New American Commentary 10. Nashville: Broadman & Holman, 2001.

Brown, Scott T. *A Weed in the Church: How A Culture of Age Segregation Is Destroying the Younger Generation, Fragmenting the Family, and Dividing the Church.* Wake Forest, NC: National Center for Family Integrated Churches, 2011.

Burger, Steve. "It Takes a Congregation...to Nurture Children." *Reformed Worship* 76 (2005). https://www.reformedworship.org/article/june-2005/it-takes-congregationto-nurture-children.

Castleman, Robbie. *Parenting in the Pew: Guiding Your Children into the Joy of Worship.* Rev. ed. Downers Grove, IL: IVP, 2013.

Christensen, Duane L. *Deuteronomy 1–11.* Word Biblical Commentary 6a. Dallas: Word, 1991.

———. *Deuteronomy 21:10—34:12.* Word Biblical Commentary 6b. Grand Rapids: Zondervan, 1997.

Cochran, George Willard, Jr., and Brian C. Richardson. "Why Your Child's Brain Needs Family Ministry." In *Trained in the Fear of God: Family Ministry in Theological, Historical, and Practical Perspective,* edited by Randy Stinson and Timothy Paul Jones, 211–220. Grand Rapids: Kregel Academic, 2011.

Craigie, Peter C. *Psalms 1–50.* Word Biblical Commentary 19. Waco, TX: Word, 1983.

Crawford, Ray, Jr. "For All Generations: The Experience and Expression of Intergenerational Worship." DMin project, Drew University, 2007.

Crider, Joseph R. *Scripture-Guided Worship: A Call to Pastors and Worship Leaders.* Fort Worth, TX: Seminary Hill, 2021.

Crowe, Brandon D. "The Trinity and the Gospel of Matthew." In *The Essential Trinity: New Testament Foundations and Practical Relevance,* edited by Brandon D. Crowe and Carl R. Trueman, 25–43. Phillipsburg, NJ: P&R, 2017.

Csinos, David M., and Ivy Beckwith. "Better Together: The Formative Power of Intergenerational Community." *Journal of Family and Community Ministries* 28 (2015) 32–47.

———. *Children's Ministry in the Way of Jesus.* Downers Grove, IL: IVP, 2013.

Frame, John M. *A History of Western Philosophy and Theology.* Phillipsburg, NJ: P&R, 2015.

Garland, Diana R. *Family Ministry: A Comprehensive Guide.* 2nd ed. Downers Grove, IL: IVP Academic, 2012.

Garrett, Duane. *A Commentary on Exodus.* Kregel Exegetical Library. Grand Rapids: Kregel Academic, 2013.

Glassford, Darwin. "Fostering an Intergenerational Culture." In *The Church of All Ages: Generations Worshiping Together,* edited by Howard Vanderwell, 71–93. Herndon, VA: Alban Institute, 2008.

Harkness, Allan. "Intergenerational and Homogeneous-Age Education: Mutually Exclusive Strategies for Faith Communities?" *Religious Education* 95 (2000) 51–63.

———. "Intergenerational Corporate Worship as a Significant Educational Activity." *Christian Education Journal* 7 (2003) 5–21.

Harwood, Adam, and Kevin E. Lawson, eds. *Infants and Children in the Church: Five Views on Theology and Ministry.* Nashville: B&H Academic, 2017.

Bibliography

Haynes, Brian. *The Legacy Path: Discover Intentional Spiritual Parenting.* Nashville: Randall House, 2011.

———. *Shift: What It Takes to Finally Reach Families Today.* Loveland, CO: Group, 2009.

Henry, Matthew. *Acts to Revelation.* Vol. 6 of *Matthew Henry's Commentary on the Whole Bible.* Peabody, MA: Hendrickson, 1991.

———. *Building A God Centered Family: A Father's Manual.* Edited by Scott Brown. Wake Forest, NC: Merchant Adventures, 2010.

———. *Genesis to Deuteronomy.* Vol. 1 of *Matthew Henry's Commentary on the Whole Bible.* Peabody, MA: Hendrickson, 1991.

———. *Isaiah to Malachi.* Vol. 4 of *Matthew Henry's Commentary on the Whole Bible.* Peabody, MA: Hendrickson, 1991.

———. *Job to Song of Solomon.* Vol. 3 of *Matthew Henry's Commentary on the Whole Bible.* Peabody, MA: Hendrickson, 1991.

———. *Joshua to Esther.* Vol. 2 of *Matthew Henry's Commentary on the Whole Bible.* Peabody, MA: Hendrickson, 1991.

———. *Matthew to John.* Vol. 5 of *Matthew Henry's Commentary on the Whole Bible.* Peabody, MA: Hendrickson, 1991.

Hess, Richard S., and M. Daniel Carroll R., eds. *Family in the Bible: Exploring Customs, Culture, and Context.* Grand Rapids: Baker Academic, 2003.

Hilborn, David, and Matt Bird, eds. *God and the Generations: Youth, Age and the Church Today: A Report by the Evangelical Alliance (UK) Commissions on Unity and Truth Among Evangelicals.* Carlisle, UK: Paternoster, 2002.

Houston, Whitney. "Greatest Love of All." Track 9 on *Whitney Houston*, lyrics by Linda Creed, produced by Michael Masser. Arista Records, 1985.

Hyde, Daniel R. *The Nursery of the Holy Spirit: Welcoming Children in Worship.* Eugene, OR: Wipf and Stock, 2014.

Jones, Timothy Paul, ed. *Perspectives on Family Ministry: Three Views.* Nashville: B&H Academic, 2009.

Leafblad, Bruce. "Philosophy of Church Music." Lecture in Philosophy of Church Music, Southwestern Baptist Theological Seminary, Fort Worth, TX, fall 1992.

Lincoln, Andrew T. *Ephesians.* Word Biblical Commentary 42. Dallas: Word, 1990.

Magruder, Jana. *Nothing Less: Engaging Kids in a Lifetime of Faith.* Nashville: LifeWay Christian Resources, 2017.

Malefyt, Norma deWaal, and Howard Vanderwell. "Reaching All Generations in Worship." *Clergy Journal* 83 (2006) 11–13.

Maslow, Abraham H. *A Theory of Human Motivation.* Mumbai, India: Sanage, 2020.

Mast, Stan. "One Congregation's Story." In *The Church of All Ages: Generations Worshiping Together*, edited by Howard Vanderwell, 129–46. Herndon, VA: Alban Institute, 2008.

May, Scottie, et al. *Children Matter: Celebrating Their Place in the Church, Family, and Community.* Grand Rapids: Eerdmans, 2005.

Menconi, Peter. *The Intergenerational Church: Understanding Congregations from WWII to www.com.* Littleton, CO: Mt. Sage, 2010.

Merriam-Webster. "Communion." Last updated September 10, 2025. https://www.merriam-webster.com/dictionary/communion.

———. "Reciprocity." Last updated August 23, 2025. https://www.merriam-webster.com/dictionary/reciprocity.

Bibliography

Merrill, Eugene H. *A Commentary on 1 & 2 Chronicles*. Kregel Exegetical Library. Grand Rapids: Kregel Academic, 2015.

Pendergraft, Robert Brian. "A Credobaptist Defense for Including Children in Corporate Worship Through a Biblically Appropriate Application of Developmental Psychology." PhD diss., Southwestern Baptist Theological Seminary, 2015.

———. "It's Not Just About the Children." Lecture presented at the Intergenerational Worship Summit at the University of Mary Hardin-Baylor, Belton, TX, January 23, 2020.

Penner, Marv. *Youth Worker's Guide to Parent Ministry*. Grand Rapids: Zondervan, 2003.

Powell, Kara, et al. "Put Away the Skinny Jeans: A Study of 250 Congregations Suggest That Engaging Youth and Young Adults Has Little to Do with Style and Everything to Do with Substance." *Christianity Today* 60 (2016) 53–58.

Rainer, Thom S., and Eric Geiger. *Simple Church: Returning to God's Process for Making Disciples*. Nashville: B&H, 2006.

Richards, Sam. "Walking Together: Intergenerational Church." *Reform Magazine* (2018) 30–31.

Roberto, John. "Our Future Is Intergenerational." *Christian Education Journal* 9 (2012) 105–20.

Rosner, Brian S. "Paul and the Trinity." In *The Essential Trinity: New Testament Foundations and Practical Relevance*, edited by Brandon D. Crowe and Carl R. Trueman, 118–34. Phillipsburg, NJ: P&R, 2017.

Ross, Allen P. *A Commentary on the Psalms*. 3 vols. Kregel Exegetical Library. Grand Rapids: Kregel Academic, 2011.

———. *Recalling the Hope of Glory: Biblical Worship from the Garden to the New Creation*. Grand Rapids: Kregel Academic, 2006.

Schultz, Samuel J. *The Old Testament Speaks*. 3rd ed. San Francisco: Harper & Row, 1980.

Shepherd, Michael B. *A Commentary on the Book of the Twelve: The Minor Prophets*. Kregel Exegetical Library. Grand Rapids: Kregel Academic, 2018.

Shirley, Chris. *Family Ministry and the Church: A Leader's Guide for Ministry Through Families*. Nashville: Randall House, 2018.

Smith, Christian, and Melinda Lundquist Denton. *Soul Searching: The Religious and Spiritual Lives of American Teenagers*. New York: Oxford University Press, 2005.

Smith, Christian, and Patricia Snell. *Souls in Transition: The Religious & Spiritual Lives of Emerging Adults*. New York: Oxford University Press, 2009.

Smith, Gordon T. "Generation to Generation: Inter-Generationality and Spiritual Formation in Christian Community." *Journal of Spiritual Formation and Soul Care* 10 (2017) 182–93.

Staats, Linda. "Walking Beside Each Other." In *InterGenerate: Transforming Churches Through Intergenerational Ministry*, edited by Holly Allen, 221–29. Abilene, TX: Abilene Christian University Press, 2018.

Stinson, Randy, and Timothy Paul Jones, eds. *Trained in the Fear of God: Family Ministry in Theological, Historical, and Practical Perspective*. Grand Rapids: Kregel Academic and Professional, 2011.

Stonehouse, Catherine, and Scottie May. *Listening to Children on the Spiritual Journey: Guidance for Those Who Teach and Nurture*. Grand Rapids: Baker Academic, 2010.

Strother, Jay. "Family-Equipping Ministry: Church and Home as Cochampions." In *Perspectives on Family Ministry: Three Views*, edited by Timothy Paul Jones, 140–67. Nashville: B&H Academic, 2009.

Bibliography

Tate, Marvin E. *Psalms 51–100*. Word Biblical Commentary 20. Grand Rapids: Zondervan, 1991.

Torrance, James B. *Worship, Community, and the Triune God of Grace*. Downers Grove, IL: IVP Academic, 1996.

Trueblood, Ben. *Within Reach: The Power of Small Changes in Keeping Students Connected*. Nashville: LifeWay, 2018.

Vanderwell, Howard, ed. *The Church of All Ages: Generations Worshiping Together*. Herndon, VA: Alban Institute, 2008.

———. "Worship Across the Generations." *Liturgy* 24 (2009) 4–10.

Vygotsky, Lev. *Mind in Society: The Development of Higher Psychological Processes*. Cambridge: Harvard University Press, 1974.

Webber, Robert E., ed. *The Biblical Foundations of Christian Worship*. Complete Library of Christian Worship 1. Peabody, MA: Hendrickson, 1993.

White, James W. *Intergenerational Religious Education*. Birmingham: Religious Education, 1988.

Whittaker, Will. *Cultivating Intergenerational Worship: Developing Corporate Worship for All Ages*. Dallas: GC2, 2022.

Witvliet, John. Foreword to *The Nursery of the Holy Spirit: Welcoming Children in Worship*, by Daniel R. Hyde, ix–x. Eugene, OR: Wipf & Stock, 2014.

Yarnell, Malcolm B., III. *God the Trinity: Biblical Portraits*. Nashville: B&H Academic, 2016.

York, Terry W. "Cross-Generational Worship." *Journal of Family Ministry* 16 (2002) 33–46.

www.ingramcontent.com/pod-product-compliance
Lightning Source LLC
Chambersburg PA
CBHW072137160426
43197CB00012B/2142